Journey

to the

Heart

of

Jesus

A Bible Study and Meditation

for Christians

by R.L. Geiger, RN, BSN

WestBow
PRESS
A DIVISION OF THOMAS NELSON

WestBow Press books may be ordered through booksellers or by contacting:

WestBow Press
A Division of Thomas Nelson
1663 Liberty Drive
Bloomington, IN 47403
www.westbowpress.com
1-(866) 928-1240

Because of the dynamic nature of the Internet, any web addresses or links contained in this book may have changed since publication and may no longer be valid. The views expressed in this work are solely those of the author and do not necessarily reflect the views of the publisher, and the publisher hereby disclaims any responsibility for them.

Any people depicted in stock imagery provided by Thinkstock are models, and such images are being used for illustrative purposes only.

Certain stock imagery © Thinkstock.

Cover illustration is a depiction of The Miracle of Lanciano by Brian C. Marine.

ISBN: 978-1-4497-4136-5 (sc)
ISBN: 978-1-4497-4137-2 (e)

Library of Congress Control Number: 2012903208

Printed in the United States of America

WestBow Press rev. date: 03/27/2012

Thank You

This Bible study was written with permission from St. Paul's Center for Biblical Theology, Dr. Scott Hahn, and San Juan Seminars, Jim Burnham, and Father Frank Chacon. It is with my deepest gratitude that I give them thanks for all they have taught me; I soak it up like a sponge ☺. I also give thanks to: Rick Warren for a "Purpose"; Lee Strobel for a "Case"; Colton Burpo for telling the world about Jesus; my spiritual mother, Jill Klontz, who taught me that Jesus loves me; Msgr. Dale Fushek who showed me Jesus in the Eucharist; my mom, Kathleen Graham, and dad, Arthur L. Geiger, for all their love and support; my children Brandon, Sam, Sierra, Dillon, Nicholas, and TJ for all their blessings, love and support and their dad, Kevin Balousek, for being the dad they love; Fr. Charlie Goraieb for his love and sincerity and his life-giving inspiration; my best friend Darla Dillaha for sharing life with me; my awesome Roommate, Jan Stevens, for her love and always being there to help and encourage me; Momma Carole Angel for her stealthy encouragement; my sister Sharon Leslie Graham for all her love and support; my brother and sister-in-law, Karl and Cheyenne Geiger, for all their love and support; Big Mike Wickham for being "a commercial brought to me by God"; my stepmom, Janice Geiger, for loving me; my stepdad, Richard Graham, for loving me; my sister units, Cyndi DelPriore and Brigit Adams, for all their love and encouragement; my best friend Erin Casey O'Connor for loving me forever; my supervisor, Darla Hill, for always encouraging me in my writings, "I just love reading your notes!"; all of the McCarthys whose love makes the world go 'round; my Aunt Janet and her whole Breaux bunch, I love my family☺; Eva Lorane and Mom at Victory Home Care for all they have blessed me; Melissa Rodriguez whose friendship and love endure forever; Mary Sue Simmons for her love and always being my buddy; Sophia Phillips for being a witness and support to me; Rebekah Divall for her love and friendship; Lily Forney for showing me grace in motion; and everyone at WestBow Press who worked on this project with me including: Danielle Chuidioni, Amanda Parsons, and Jason Klarke you rock!

Dedication

This Bible study is dedicated with all my love to:

Jill Klontz,

Darla Dillaha,

My mom and dad

And

All of the McCarthys☺

Also with thanks to:

Rick Warren, Lee Strobel, and Colton Burpo

Purpose of Study

The Bible is holy, it is inspired by God and it is a rich fountain overflowing with truth. As we drink from this fountain we come to know and love Jesus Christ, who came to fulfill God's plan for life. The purpose of this Bible Study is to bring you deeper into communion with Jesus Christ, our Lord and Savior, by guiding you right to His heart. It is crucial that we receive the heart of Jesus; from the heart of Jesus comes the pulse of life.

The readings are brief so work it daily—one day at a time. Read it in the morning and then meditate on the short verse as a prayer throughout the day. It is important that you meditate on the Scripture verse each day, as this will bring you into deeper union with God by absorbing the Scriptures. At the end of each chapter is a brief homework assignment which will help to increase your understanding of the material read. Work this study in a small group for fellowship and discussion opportunities. My prayer for you as you work the study is that you hunger for Truth and thirst for the Word. May God bless you as you seek to know Him better.

Journey to the Heart of Jesus:

A Bible Study and Meditation for Christians

Contents

Week 1: The Word Creates   1

Day 1: In the Beginning   3

Day 2: Creation in Covenant   5

Day 3: Covenant with Noah   8

Day 4: Covenant with Abraham   10

Day 5: Covenant with Moses   12

Day 6: Covenant with David   14

Day 7: The New Covenant   16

Week 2: Sacrifices of the Old Covenant   23

Day 1: Cain and Abel   25

Day 2: Noah's Sacrifice   27

Day 3: Melchizedek Blesses Abraham   29

Day 4: Sublime Obedience of Abraham   31

Day 5: Passover Regulations   33

Day 6: Sacrifices of Leviticus   35

Day 7: David's Sacrifice and Reverence for the Ark   37

Week 3:   The Word Becomes Flesh   45

Day 1: And Dwelt Among Us   47

Day 2: Mediator of a Superior Covenant   50

Day 3: The New Canticle   51

Day 4: Listen to Him   53

Day 5: Do Whatever He Tells You   55

Day 6: Obedience of Faith   58

Day 7: Let's Eat!   60

Week 4:   Flesh for Salvation   67

Day 1: Jesus Feeds Five Thousand   69

Day 2: Jesus Walks on Water   71

Day 3: Faith Alone   73

Day 4: Bread of Life   75

Day 5: Flesh to Eat?   78

Day 6: Too Hard to Accept   80

Day 7: Eat My Flesh   83

Week 5: The Last Supper Delivers   89

     Day 1: Blood of the New Covenant   91

     Day 2: The Christian Passover   95

     Day 3: Lamb of God   97

     Day 4: Once for All   99

     Day 5: The Passover Lamb   101

     Day 6: Fulfillment of the Law   104

     Day 7: Body and Blood   107

Week 6: Back to the Word   113

     Day 1: Teachings Handed Down   115

     Day 2: Built on a Rock   124

     Day 3: High Priest Forever   128

     Day 4: Feed My Sheep   131

     Day 5: Authority of the Holy Church   134

     Day 6: One Body   137

     Day 7: Foundation of Truth   144

Week 7: The Sacrifice of the Lamb   155

     Day 1: Love the Lord   157

     Day 2: Love One Another   159

     Day 3: The Agony in the Garden   161

Day 4: The Scourging at the Pillar   163

Day 5: The Crowning with Thorns   165

Day 6: The Carrying of the Cross   168

Day 7: The Crucifixion: To Seven Himself   171

Week 1

The Word Creates

Week 1: The Word Creates

Day 1

In the Beginning

Read: Genesis chapter 1

Memorize/meditate: Genesis 1:3

"Then God Said, 'Let there be light,' and there was light." (NABRE)

In the story of the creation of the universe notice how God's word *becomes* what it declares, i.e. "Let there be light" and there was light. God's word is so powerful that when He makes a declaration, the thing that He declares actually comes into being. Since God is truth, when He speaks truth issues forth:

His declaration = Reality

Because

God = Truth

Notice also the divine order in which He creates with purpose. In the beginning the world was *formless and empty* so God goes about creating *form* and *matter.* The creation story describes a definite organization in God's progression of events.

On the first 3 days he created *form* because the world was *formless:*

Day 1: day and night

Day 2: sky and seas

Day 3: land and vegetation

On the next 3 days He created *matter* to rule each form because the world was *empty:*

Day 4: sun to rule the day; moon to rule the night

Day 5: birds to rule the sky; fish to rule the seas

Day 6: man to rule the land; animals to rule the vegetation

The perfect order in His divine plan for creating the world can also be seen in the content and unity of scripture. When we read the books of the Bible according to God's saving plan for the world, we see that all of the books fall into place in perfect order according to His work.

Week 1: In the Beginning

Day 2

Creation in Covenant

Read: Genesis 2:1-4

Memorize/meditate: Genesis 2:3

"So God blessed the seventh day and made it holy, because on it he rested from all the work he had done in creation." (NABRE)

The fact that God rested on the seventh day is significant to creation because it is this day that forms the covenant bond which hallows all of creation. God was finished with His work on the sixth day and then He *went on to make a seventh day.* It is through the existence of the seventh day that God *binds* Himself to His creation. The seventh day is hallowed; it is blessed because it brings God into covenant relation with His creation forming a unique family bond. A covenant is an exchange of persons to bind themselves together in a familial relationship, for example a marriage. Covenants make families. In creating day seven God transforms His relationship with man from that of *Creator* to that of *Father.*

A covenant is made by swearing an oath, and in the Hebrew language the word for "to swear an oath" translates into English as "to seven oneself". Every time a Hebrew would swear an oath, they would literally say, "I seven myself . . ."; therefore, it is by virtue of the seventh day that God "sevens Himself" with His creation, thus becoming bound in a familial relationship with man, He is their Father and they are His children. As their Father, God gives them specific instructions, which they did not heed, unfortunately, thereby breaking their covenant oath with their Father and causing spiritual death. This is what is referred to as the stain of Original Sin. It was the first sin committed by humans, therefore it is original, and it is a stain, because it is passed on to our souls at birth; so it has stained mankind.

God reveals Himself to us in Holy Scripture, and the Bible is all about the covenant—the Old and the New. It is through our covenant with God that he leads us to salvation, back home to Him. The Bible tells us salvation history—the history of how God has brought His people to salvation by means of a covenant oath. The greatest theologian of the early Christian Church, Irenaeus, stated that when reading the Bible "Understanding . . . consists in showing why there are a number of covenants with mankind and in teaching what is the character of those covenants." (Against Heresies, Book 1, chapter 10, no. 3) It is by reading the Bible that we learn about God, and it is through the character of the covenants in the Bible that God reveals Himself to us.

Week 1: In the Beginning

Day 3

Covenant with Noah

Read: Genesis 9:8-17

Memorize/meditate: Genesis 9:13

"I set my bow in the clouds to serve as a sign of the covenant between me and the earth." (NABRE)

God's covenant oath with Noah is in the sign of a rainbow. Notice that the rainbow is made up of *seven* colors. God has led Noah and his family through the flood safely and has renewed His covenant bond with man through Noah. As Adam was the mediator of the original covenant, Noah is the mediator of the renewed covenant. The covenant with Adam was inclusive of a married couple and the renewal is now extended to the form of a family, Noah's nuclear family of husband, wife, and children. You will notice that the series of covenants between God and man which are recorded in the Bible, build upon each other to gradually increase God's family. You will also notice that the covenants of the Old Testament are symbols which reach their culmination and fulfillment in the New and everlasting Covenant of Jesus Christ, which is recorded in the New Testament. In other words, the covenants of the Old Testament are symbols which are actualized in the New Testament. For example, in 1Pet 3:20-21 we read that God's covenant with Noah prefigures baptism. We see that Noah was saved from the waters of the Flood, but his soul was not actually saved only his earthly life was delivered. In the New Covenant of our Lord Jesus Christ, our souls are *actually and truly saved* by the waters of baptism. The waters of baptism wash away the stain of Original Sin which was committed by Adam and Eve upon breaking their covenant oath with God. The Flood of the Old Covenant is a symbol for what is actualized by baptism in the New Covenant.

Old Covenant = symbol

New Covenant = reality

Week 1: In the Beginning

Day 4

Covenant with Abraham

Read: Genesis 17: 1-14

Memorize/meditate: Genesis 17:4

"My covenant with you is this: you are to become the father of a host of nations." (NABRE)

The stain of Original Sin is passed on through the procreation of man and people continue to sin and break the covenant bond with God, so God continues to renew His covenant oath with man through a series of mediators in the Old Testament. God establishes His renewed covenant now with the patriarch Abraham, and the sign of the covenant is circumcision. Through His covenant with Abraham God now extends His family bond beyond the form of a nuclear family to the form of tribes. God promises that Abraham will be a father of many nations and that kings shall stem from him, which is a foreshadow of Jesus Christ who is the King of kings (Rev19:16) and is recorded as "the son of David, the son of Abraham" in Matt 1:1, the very first line of the New Testament. God makes three promises to Abraham: to make him a great nation; to give him a great name; and to make him the source of blessing for all of the world. God kept all three promises he made to Abraham. If God says it—**it happens**. Remember from Day 1 of this study:

His declaration = Reality

Week 1: In the Beginning

Day 5

Covenant with Moses

Read: Exodus chapter 12; 19:4-6

Memorize/meditate: Exodus 12:27

"This is the Passover sacrifice of the Lord, who passed over the houses of the Israelites in Egypt; when he struck down the Egyptians, he spared our houses." (NABRE)

When God came into covenant relationship with Moses the sign of the covenant was the Passover meal. The Passover was a sacrifice and a meal shared by God's chosen people. In this covenant relationship God extended His family from tribe to nation, and we see in the character of God's relationship with the nation of Israel a fatherly care as He leads them out of slavery in Egypt into the promised land: He saves His children (Ex 12:29-31), clothes them (Ex 12:35-36), guides them (Ex 13:21-22), feeds them (Ex 16:1-17), protects them

(Ex 14:10-29; 17:8-16), teaches them (Ex 20: 1-17; 21), and lives with them (Ex 25:8; 40: 34-38). Notice again how the covenants in salvation history unfold to progressively include more people. Notice also that while each covenant has included more people progressively, they have all been mediated by only one man. So the covenant between God and His people is once again renewed, this time through the mediation of Moses and as a sign of the covenant with the Lord, the people must eat the flesh of the sacrificed Passover lamb and sprinkle the blood of the lamb over their doorposts with a bunch of Hyssop in order to be spared from death. This is the Passover sacrifice of the Lord and this Passover meal foreshadows the events to come in the New Covenant/Testament.

Week 1: In the Beginning

Day 6

Covenant with David

Read: 2Samuel 7:8-16; 23:5; Psalm 89:1-5, 27-30, 35-38

Memorize/meditate: Psalm 89:28

"And I will make him the first-born, highest of the kings of the earth." (NABRE)

The covenant between God and David is a fulfillment of God's covenant with Abraham (Gen 17:6). It is also a foreshadowing promise of the kingdom to come—the eternal kingdom of God. This covenant renewal which is mediated by David has opened God's salvation plan to His people beyond a nation now and into a Kingdom, and it is the last covenant between God and His people in the Old Testament. The sign of God's covenant w David is the throne. God's promises to David include: establishing David's kingdom as a dynasty; David's son will rule over his kingdom and his kingdom shall be forever; David's son will build a temple for the Ark of the Covenant; David's son will be adopted as God's own son (This is the first time that an *individual* is referred to as God's own son since Adam. After Adam God referred only to the whole nation of Israel as His first-born son.); if David's son breaks God's Law, God will punish him, but He will not disown him as He disowned Saul, the king who preceded David; and finally, that David's dynasty will never end, there will always be an heir of David seated on his throne.

Recall again from the study on Day One how powerful God's word is; that it **does** what it declares. Take a moment now to reflect on the truths purveyed through each covenant oath God swore with His people through Adam, Noah, Abraham, Moses, and David. Upon studying and reading the Bible in depth, you see that God keeps all of His promises—again, by the power of His word—that which He says **actually happens.**

Week 1: In the Beginning

Day 7

The New Covenant

Read: Jeremiah 31: 31-34; Matthew 1;1; Mark 1:1; Luke 22:14-20; Revelation 5:9-10

Memorize/meditate: Jeremiah 31:33b

"I will place my law within them and write it upon their hearts; I will be their God and they shall be my people." (NABRE)

The prophet Jeremiah foretold of the coming of the New Covenant which would be internal, **inside them.** His people would receive the law of the covenant **within** them. With the coming of the New Covenant God opens His family bond beyond a kingdom, beyond "every tribe and tongue, people and nation"—the New Covenant is *universal,* for *everyone.* It is the culmination and the fulfillment of all of the covenants in the Old Testament and it is mediated by God himself who came in the flesh of Jesus Christ. The sign of the New

Covenant is the flesh and blood of Jesus Christ, the Son of God the Father, and the sign will be *within* His people making the New Covenant superior to the Old Covenant. Jesus is the mediator of the New Covenant; He is at once both the High Priest *and* the Lamb of sacrifice of the New Covenant for all eternity. All who are in the New Covenant are a kingdom for God—a kingdom and priests who will reign on earth.

Homework

For

Week 1

1.)   Write the dictionary definition for the following words:

actualize-

_____

_____

bond-

_____

_____

covenant-

_____

_____

image-

_____

_____

likeness-

_____

_____

mediator-

_____

_____

oath-

_____

_____

patriarch-

_____

_____

reality-

_____

_____

salvation-

_____

_____

swear-

_____

_____

symbol-

_____

_____

testament-

_____

_____

truth-

_____

_____

universal-

_____

_____

2.) Refer to Genesis chapter 1, God creates everything by saying, "Let there be . . ." How does the terminology differ in the creation of man and what is the significance of this change?

_____

_____

_____

3.) What does it mean to be created in God's "image and likeness"?

_____

_____

_____

4.) Do you take special time to honor God as your Father? Give examples.

_____

_____

_____

5.) Explain the differences between a marriage and a business partnership. One is a covenant and one is a contract, explain.

_____

_____

_____

6.)   God the Father prescribed the ritual for the Passover as a memorial meal in Exodus chapter 12. What happened to those who were not of the covenant or did not keep the commands of the covenant?

_____

_____

_____

7.)   How did Adam break the covenant between him and God the Father? See Genesis 2:15-17; 3:1-7

_____

_____

_____

Week 2

Sacrifices of the Old Covenant

Week 2: Sacrifices of the Old Covenant

Day 1

Cain and Abel

Read Genesis 4: 1-8

Memorize/meditate: Genesis 4:4

". . . while Abel, for his part, brought one of the best firstlings of his flock. The Lord looked with favor on Abel and his offering . . ." (NABRE)

This is the first mention of sacrifice in the Bible. Notice how important the sacrifice is to the Lord; He was pleased with Abel's offering, because Abel honored Him by offering his best gift while Cain did not. The Lord was pleased with the disposition of Abel's heart and displeased with the disposition of Cain's heart. Abel's good and worthy sacrifice showed God that He was more important to Abel than Abel was to himself.

The necessity of the sacrifice was brought about by Adam's Original Sin in Genesis 3:6. In disobeying God's command Adam took a lateral move and ignored the authority above him, seeing himself and his decision as more important than obeying the command of his Father. After Original Sin was brought into the world by Adam and Eve we see hereafter a series of sacrifices in which God's people seek atonement for sin. The Lord tells Cain that he *can be the master* of his own sin, but the *sin masters him* instead, and he is driven to murder out of his jealousy for Abel.

Week 2: Sacrifices of the Old Covenant

Day 2

Noah's Sacrifice

Read: Genesis 8:15-22

Memorize/meditate: Genesis 8:20

"Then Noah built an altar to the Lord, and choosing from every clean animal and every clean bird, he offered holocausts on the altar." (NABRE)

This is the climax of the great flood which destroyed all life on earth— all the life that God wanted to destroy, but Noah found favor with the Lord (Gen 6:7-8). So God protects Noah and his family, as a good Father, while He wipes out all other life on earth. The sin of Adam had snowballed so badly that God sent a flood to destroy life and preserved a favored family to renew life in goodness upon the earth. When they were delivered safely from the flood, Noah acknowledged, honored, and paid respects to God his Father by building an altar and offering sacrifices to Him. Noah worshipped and God was pleased;

He vowed mercy on His creation because of Noah's sacrifice. It is by offering good and worthy sacrifices to the Lord that Noah keeps his own heart cleansed. Recall the words God said to Cain, "sin is a demon lurking at the door: his urge is toward you, yet you can be his master." Unfortunately, though, as salvation history unfolds God's people continue to fall from grace.

Week 2: Sacrifices of the Old Covenant

Day 3

Melchizedek Blesses Abraham

Read: Genesis 14: 18-20; Psalm 110:4

Memorize/meditate: Genesis 14:18

"Melchizedek, king of Salem, brought out bread and wine, and being a priest of God Most High, he blessed Abram . . ." (NABRE)

Melchizedek is an extremely powerful figure in salvation history. The name "Melchizedek" means "King of Righteousness" in the Hebrew and Canaanite languages. Melchizedek is a priest and the king of Salem who blesses Abram (name not yet changed to Abraham which happens in Gen 17:5). His blessing invokes the name of God and is imparted with an act of faith in a basic creed format, ". . . God Most High, the creator of heaven and earth . . . God Most high, who delivered your foes into your hand." He recognizes God as Almighty who is both Creator and Redeemer. This blessing from Melchizedek is so powerful that Abraham then gives him a tenth of everything. This is the first time in the Bible that an event of tithing is recorded. Abraham gives Melchizedek a tenth of everything *without hesitation*, and in doing so Abraham shows that he recognizes Melchizedek as his superior, in which it naturally follows that all of Abraham's progeny will be under Melchizedek as well.

While animal sacrifice for atonement is recorded over and over again in the Old Testament, it is this sacrificial offering of *bread and wine* which brings about a powerful blessing upon the patriarch of Abraham resulting in his offer of a tithe. This points us further towards the New Covenant which involves the sacrificial offering of bread and wine by Jesus, also a king and priest by the order of Melchizedek (Ps 110:4).

As an interesting note, we as Christians believe in God as the Holy Trinity—the Father, Son, and Holy Spirit. In Genesis 1:26 we find the first hint of the entity of the Holy Trinity, "Let us make man . . ." If Jesus was in the beginning with God and Jesus IS God, then who preceded who in the line of priests by the order of Melchizedek: Melchizedek or Jesus?

Week 2: Sacrifices of the Old Covenant

Day 4

Sublime Obedience of Abraham

Read: Genesis 22:1-19

Memorize/meditate: Genesis 22:16b-17a

". . . because you acted as you did in not withholding from me your beloved son, I will bless you abundantly and make your descendants as countless as the stars of the sky . . ." (NABRE)

Abraham was obedient to God's command to sacrifice his beloved son. Here we see complete submission in Abraham by following through with the Lord's command without questioning it. Abraham shows his love for God the father by his *obedience of faith*. In the sacrifice of the New Covenant, Jesus is also obedient to the Father without question. There are other observable similarities between the sacrifice of Isaac and the sacrifice of Jesus. Abraham's son carries the wood for his sacrifice just as Jesus carries the wood for His sacrifice, His cross (Jn 19:17). Abraham treks up Mount Moriah for 3 days knowing that his destination is to sacrifice his son, but on the third day his son is saved. In the New Testament Jesus dies on Calvary (Jn 19:17), one of the hills of Mount Moriah, and is resurrected on the third day (Lk 24:6-7). God spared Abraham from the pain of sacrificing his son in the Old Covenant, but in the fulfillment of the New Covenant God endured the pain of sacrificing His own beloved Son.

Week 2: Sacrifices of the Old Covenant

Day 5

Passover Regulations

Read: Exodus 12:1-20, 43-51

Memorize/meditate: Exodus 12:46

"It must be eaten in one and the same house; you may not take any of its flesh outside the house. You shall not break any of its bones." (NABRE)

The Passover sacrifice was given specifications by the Lord. One must be in the covenant to celebrate the Passover feast. The food of the feast was the sacrificed lamb itself. Of all the Old Testament sacrifices, this was the only sacrifice which was eaten as a perpetual, memorial meal, and there was a ritual prescribed as to how it was to be eaten: ". . . with your loins girt, sandals on your feet and your staff in hand, you shall eat like those who are in flight" (Ex 12:11). It was this sacrifice of the unblemished lamb that saved the first-born of those who were in the covenant family of God, and the sacrificed lamb *must be eaten* by those who were in the covenant to be saved. **It must be eaten.**

Week 2: Sacrifices of the Old Covenant

Day 6

Sacrifices of Leviticus

Read: Leviticus 1:1-5; 3:1,2; 4:1-6; 5:5-10; 6:22; 7:2; 8:1-15; 20:7,8; 20:26

Memorize/meditate: Leviticus 20:7

"Sanctify yourselves then and be holy; for I, the Lord, your God, am holy." (NABRE)

In the sacrifices of Leviticus we see that the laws contained therein serve to teach the Israelites that they should always keep themselves in a state of purity through sacrifice as a sign of their intimate union with the Lord. This is the resounding theme in the book of Leviticus; "you shall be holy, because I the Lord am holy." Notice how exact He is in prescribing the rituals for sacrifice, i.e. some blood is to be sprinkled on the altar, some blood is to be poured out—there is precision to the ritual of the sacrifices He prescribes. The Lord even *warns* them to *keep the rituals* for purity which he prescribes (Lev 20:8).

Notice also the "plot" of the book of Leviticus: the priestly order of the tribe of Levi which carries out the orders of the Lord. Here we also see exactitude in the ritual of organization as described in chapter 8. Recall the organization of the creation of the world from Week 1 Day 1 of this study. God works within a definite framework of order and organization. We even see echoes of the power of "seven" in Leviticus as some of the sacrificial blood must be sprinkled on the altar **"seven times"** and the ordination ceremony itself lasted **"seven days"** (Lev 8:33).

Week 2: Sacrifices of the Old Covenant

Day 7

David's Sacrifice and Reverence for the Ark

Read: 2Samuel 6:1-18

Memorize/meditate: 2Sam 6:18

"When he finished making these offerings, he blessed the people in the name of the Lord of hosts." (NABRE)

David sought the ark of the Lord which had not been addressed in the reign of his predecessor, Saul. The ark is so holy that Uzzah was struck down for touching it (2Sam 6:7). We see the harsh consequences of Liturgical abuse here. There are 2 infractions to the rules in the sequence of events with the ark: 1.) The ark was riding on an ox-cart instead of being carried by priests on two poles (Ex 25:14-15); 2.) There was a soldier next to the ark, and only priests are allowed near it(1Chr: 14-15). When God gives instructions or prescribes rituals, He is serious!

David offers sacrifices to the Lord before the ark. He offers sacrifices before the ark advances its *seventh* step and then again after the ark enters into the City of David, Jerusalem.

Throughout the Old Testament we see that offering sacrifices to the Lord cleanses, purifies, and sanctifies man. Take a moment now to reflect on: the sin of Adam through love of self; the initiation and effect of sacrificial offering as begun by Cain and Abel; the sacrifice of Noah with whom the Lord found favor; the impact of the unusual sacrifice of Melchizedek; the effects of the sublime obedience of Abraham; the unique circumstances of the Passover sacrifice; the ordination and offertory sacrifices of the Levitical priests; the effects of liturgical abuse and the reverence of David through sacrifices before the ark.

Homework

For

Week 2

1.)   Write the dictionary definitions of the following words:

anoint-

_____

_____

appurtenance-

_____

_____

ark-

_____

_____

atonement-

_____

_____

consecrate-

_____

_____

diadem-

_____

_____

ephod-

_____

_____

gird-

_____

_____

laver-

_____

_____

Liturgical-

_____

_____

miter-

_____

_____

obedient-

_____

_____

oblation-

_____

_____

progeny-

_____

_____

reverence-

_____

_____

sacrifice-

_____

_____

sanctify-

_____

_____

sublime-

_____

_____

Urim and Thummim-

_____

_____

Vestment-

_____

_____

2.)   Who blessed Abraham and what did Abraham do after he received this

blessing?

_____

_____

_____

3.) What did God order Abraham to sacrifice and how did he respond to the order?

_____

_____

_____

4.) What was the only Old Testament sacrifice that was eaten as a memorial meal?

_____

_____

_____

5.) What did God order Moses to sacrifice and who was saved by the sacrifice?

_____

_____

_____

6.) What three items did the ark of the covenant contain that made it holy? See Exodus 16:33-34; 25:16; Numbers 17:25-26; Heb 9:4. Why was Uzzah struck down by the Lord?

_____

_____

_____

7.) Given the order and organization of sacrificial ordination ceremonies, do you think it would be possible to trace a line of priests of the order of Levi, like genealogies are traced?

_____

_____

_____

Week 3

The Word Becomes Flesh

Week 3: The Word Becomes Flesh

Day 1

And Dwelt Among Us

Read: Genesis 1:3; Exodus 3:14; Matthew 1:1: John 1:1-5, 14; John 8:58

Memorize/meditate: John 1:14a

"and the word became flesh and made his dwelling among us . . ." (NABRE)

When we come to the New Testament, we open it to the Gospel of Matthew to read that Jesus is the son of David and the son of Abraham. So He comes forth as the fulfillment of the promises made in God's covenants with David, to whom He promised an eternal kingdom, and Abraham, in whom He promised that all nations would be blessed. Luke's Gospel even traces the genealogy of Jesus all the way back to Adam (Lk 3:23-38), who was of God. In John's Gospel Jesus is equated with God in the very beginning: ". . . The Word *was* God" (Jn 1:1); referring to "the Word" as the spoken "Word" of God in

Genesis 1:3. John then goes on to testify in his Gospel that he saw Jesus, knew Jesus, believed Jesus and received grace and truth through Him.

When speaking to the Jews in John 8:58, Jesus uses the same words to name His eternal existence as God did when speaking to Moses: "I Am". In fact, notice that when Jesus makes this statement He begins with "Amen, amen". This is a form of oath swearing for the ancients. Jesus is testifying by oath that He is "I Am."

The Word of God has come in the flesh—God has come to earth *as a person*—to fulfill *all* of the prophecies of the Old Testament. He became *flesh* for us, for our salvation; He came down from heaven to reconcile us with God and through His sacrifice He allows us to participate in His divine nature (1Cor 10: 16-17). He has come to make a New Covenant with His people that would be binding and **REAL**. The covenants of the Old Testament, remember, were symbolic while the New Covenant is reality. This concept is difficult for us to grasp, but nevertheless remains true. Jesus's life and teachings remain a mystery to us even as we strive to understand them better. Let us recall Isaiah 55:8-9:

For my thoughts are not your thoughts,

Nor are your ways my ways, says the Lord.

As high as the heavens are above the earth,

So high are my ways above your ways

And my thoughts above your thoughts.

Week 3: The Word Becomes Flesh

Day 2

Mediator of a Superior Covenant

Read: Hebrews 8:6-13

Memorize/meditate: Hebrews 8:6-13

"Now he has obtained so much more excellent a ministry as he is mediator of a better covenant, enacted on better promises."(NABRE)

Jesus is the mediator of the New Covenant which is superior to the Old Covenant. The Word became flesh and made His covenant among us. The New Covenant is superior to the Old because **God himself is the mediator and the sacrifice** for it; the former covenants were mediated by *men* and included the sacrifice of *animals*. The prophecy from Isaiah says that the Lord will make a new covenant with the house of Judah; David was from the tribe of Judah, and Jesus is the son of David. With the New Covenant, the laws of the covenant will now be *inside* God's people and God will forgive and forget their sins.

Week 3: The Word Becomes Flesh

Day 3

The New Canticle

Read: 2Samuel 7:12-15; Psalm 110:1; Revelation 5:9-10

Memorize/meditate: Revelation 5:10

"You made them a kingdom and priests for our God, and they will reign on earth." (NABRE)

Jesus Christ is the Lamb of God; He was slain as a sacrifice to gain a New Covenant with God. A covenant which was established as a universal covenant: unto all tribes, tongues, people, and nations. It is now through the bond of the New Covenant, which is mediated by Jesus Christ in which we receive family relationship with God. As we read in Ephesians 1:5 ". . . he destined us for adoption to himself through Jesus Christ, in accord with the favor of his will." We are adopted as sons and daughters unto the Father by oath of the New Covenant. Remember what we learned about covenants in

Week 1 of this study? A covenant is an exchange of persons which establishes a familial relationship, and a covenant is an unbreakable bond which is made by swearing an oath.

Covenants make families.

Week 3: The Word Becomes Flesh

Day 4

Listen to Him

Read: Matthew 3:16-17; Matthew 17:5

Memorize/meditate: Matthew 17:5b

". . . then from the cloud came a voice that said, 'This is my beloved Son, with whom I am well-pleased. Listen to him.'" (NABRE)

God refers to his Son as "beloved" just as Abraham's son, Isaac, was referred to as his "beloved son" in Gen 22:12. God is Jesus's Father, and He recognizes and claims Him before witnesses. God commands those present to "listen to Him". God wants us to listen to Jesus and to obey Him. Through many trials in the Old Testament God showed the importance of obedience to His commands: to Adam, "From that tree you shall not eat . . ."; to Abraham, "Take your son Isaac . . . you shall offer him up as a holocaust . . ."; to Moses, ". . . procure lambs for your families and slaughter them as Passover victims . . ."

In these few examples of the weight of obedience to God's commands we see that there are consequences involved for disobeying them and rewards for keeping them; just as a good father always lovingly enforces his law to his children through discipline. God commands us now in the New Testament, **"This is my beloved Son . . . Listen to Him."**

Week 3: The Word Becomes Flesh

Day 5

Do Whatever He Tells You

Read: John 2:1-11

Memorize/meditate: John 2:5

"His mother said to the servers, 'Do whatever he tells you.'" (NABRE)

The story of Jesus's first miracle is demonstrative of obedience of faith on many levels: Jesus is obedient to His mother in obedience of the 4th Commandment: Honor thy father and mother (Ex 20:12); The servers are obedient to Mary and then they are obedient to Jesus; and the disciples in turn are obedient in their faith of Jesus. We could also say that His mother is being obedient to the Father in heaven, because Scripture tells us that she has given herself *entirely* to Him: "Behold, I am the Handmaid of the Lord" (Lk 1:38); and Luke 1:46-55 records the song of Mary in which she proclaims a magnificent pledge of commitment to God the Father and her *devout* faith in her unborn son by acknowledging him as the fulfillment of the promises made to Abraham and to Israel. Therefore, we know that she does **all things** in submission to the Father.

As the story of the wedding feast unfolds, Jesus's mother shows that she has complete faith in her son. When they run out of wine she tells Him what the problem is and then leaves it in his hands. Notice that she does not tell Jesus *what* to do; she only tells him the nature of the problem and gives him command to take charge, having faith that He will obey her. She then commands the servers to "Do whatever he tells you" which they obey. In His obedience to His mother, Jesus takes command of the situation and tells the servers to fill the water jars, which they obediently fill. They demonstrate their obedience to Him, notice, by not *just filling* the jars, but by filling them *all the way to the brim.* Jesus then performs his first miracle, turning the water into wine, and His disciples begin to believe in Him after seeing this miracle. Throughout the Gospel, from then on, the disciples are obedient of faith in Him and His teachings.

The Gospel tells us:

The word became flesh

And made his dwelling among us,

And his Father told us to **"Listen to him"**

And his mother told us to **"Do whatever he tells you."**

Day 6

Obedience of Faith

Read: John 3:16; 14:6; Rom 1:3-5; 16:25-27

Memorize/meditate: John 14:6

"Jesus said to him, 'I am the way, the truth, and the life. No one comes to the father except through me.'" (NABRE)

Jesus is the Way, and the Truth, and the Life. No one comes to the Father except through him. We need to believe in Him and have faith in Him and *obey* Him, because he is the Way to the Father. Just as Abraham *believed* in God, his Father, and *obeyed* Him, we also need to have that sublime obedience to Jesus's commands if we want to follow him. Jesus is the only Way to the Father, so we must follow the Way, and we do that through obedience to Him and His commands. St. Paul speaks of this obedience of faith in his letters, especially in his letter to the Romans where he opens and closes his letter with the remarks of "obedience of faith." St. Paul states that it is his duty to share the Gospel with all the Gentiles in order ". . . to bring about the obedience of faith . . ." He must dutifully pass on the traditions and teachings of the New Covenant which were given to him by the risen Lord. He must take special care to pass on these traditions to the Gentiles, because they were not previously in the Covenant. In the Old Covenant the Law of Moses belonged only to the Israelites, but the New Covenant is universal; it includes all people.

It is by our obedience of faith in God that our love for Him is made manifest. Consider our own earthly families. The father tells his son to be home by 10:00. The son shows his love for his father and is faithful to his father's authority by following the command. If the son simply says, "Father, I believe in you and I love you, but I don't want to come home at 10:00, so I'll come home when I am ready to come home." Has the son actually been faithful to his father? No, the son would be disciplined for being disobedient to the command given to him. To be faithful to Jesus Christ, the Son of God, the Way, the Truth, and the Life, we **must obey Him** as the Gospel tells us:

"Listen to Him."

"Do whatever He tells you."

Week 3: The Word Becomes Flesh

Day 7

Let's Eat!

Read: Genesis 2:15-17; 3:6; John 6:53-58

Memorize/meditate: John 6:54

"Whoever eats my flesh and drinks my blood has eternal life, and I will raise him on the last day." (NABRE)

In the beginning God created Adam and He commanded him not to eat the fruit from the tree of knowledge of good and bad. He said, "From this tree you shall not eat; the moment you eat from it you are surely doomed to die." Remember, God can not lie because when He speaks, truth issues forth. So, what happened next? There was disobedience on the part of Adam and follow-through on the threat from God (Gen 3:13-19). Adam chose to disregard the command of his Father; he made a lateral move by acting on his own desires rather than respecting the authority of the command that came from above him.

When Adam disobeyed and ate the fruit, it caused the declaration from God, "the moment you eat from it you are surely doomed to die" to become reality, and spiritual death ensued upon all of humanity as a result of Adam's sin. The tree that Adam ate from was the tree of knowledge of good and evil, and Adam has internalized the fruit of the knowledge of good and evil.

Our loving Father has a plan to save us, though, to bring us home to Him. In the fulfillment of time He sent His Son to undo what Adam has done. Notice the intimate union that Jesus is now calling us to: "Whoever eats my flesh and drinks my blood *remains in me and I in him*." (Jn 6:54) As the prophet Jeremiah foretold of the New Covenant, "I will place my law *within* them. (Jer 31:33)" While we lost eternal salvation with the Father in heaven through disobedience, we now have a promise of gaining it back through **obedience**. In the beginning, the command from God the Father was, "Eat the fruit of that tree and you shall die." In the fulfillment of time the command from God the Son is, "Eat my flesh and you shall live." By all means brothers and sisters, **let's eat!**

Homework

For

Week 3

1.)   Write the dictionary definitions for the following words:

beloved-

_____

_____

covenant-

_____

_____

darkness-

_____

_____

devout-

_____

_____

faithful-

_____

_____

flesh-

_____

_____

Gentile-

_____

_____

grace-

_____

_____

light-

_____

_____

mediator-

_____

_____

obedience-

_____

_____

submission-

_____

_____

universal-

_____

_____

2.)   The Gospel according to John equates Jesus with God and states that His presence was "in the beginning with God"; can you describe Jesus's presence in the beginning?

_____

_____

_____

3.)   Is obedience of faith important to you? In what ways are you obedient of faith? Give examples.

_____

_____

_____

4.) Adam internalized the fruit of "good and evil" (Gen 2:17; 3:6) and sin entered his heart, if we internalize the flesh of Christ what would enter our hearts? See John 1:14.

_____

_____

_____

5.) At the wedding feast in Cana, why did the servers listen to Mary?

_____

_____

_____

6.) How is the mediator of the New Covenant superior to the mediators of the Old Covenant?

_____

_____

_____

7.) Refer to Revelation 5:9, what was used for payment to purchase a universal kingdom for God?

_____

_____

_____

Week 4

Flesh for Salvation

Week 4: Flesh for Salvation

Day 1

Jesus Feeds Five Thousand

Read: John 6:1-15; Deuteronomy 18:15

Memorize/meditate: John 6:11

"Then Jesus took the loaves, gave thanks, and distributed them to those who were reclining, and also as much of the fish as they wanted." (NABRE)

The miracle of the loaves and fish happens when the Passover is near (Jn 6:4). After this Passover, Jesus only celebrated one more Passover, and it was on the night before His death. The crowd was very large, about 5,000, and Jesus fed them with 5 loaves of bread and 2 fish. We might refer to this miracle as the "multi-location" of the loaves, because the same 5 loaves fed 5,000 people. Jesus knew that He was going to work a miracle, and He drew attention to Himself and the sign He was about to work by asking Philip, "Where can we buy enough food for them to eat?" In asking Philip this question He is testing

Philip's faith, and Philip answered Him that it would basically be impossible to get enough food for the crowd. So Jesus knows that Philip thinks it is impossible for them to feed these people, and He is about to show Philip that it is not too impossible of a task for Him to handle. After performing the miracle, some of the people then speak about Him as being the prophet that Moses foretold and notice what Moses said about the prophet, again we see the command to listen to Jesus, this time from Moses: **"To him you shall listen."**

Week 4: Flesh for Salvation

Day 2

Jesus Walks on Water

Read: John 6:16-21; Matthew 14:22-33

Memorize/meditate: Jn 6:19

"When they had rowed about three or four mile, they saw Jesus walking on the sea and coming near the boat, and they began to be afraid." (NABRE)

After working a faith-invoking miracle of feeding 5,000 people with 5 loaves and 2 fish, Jesus went off to the mountain alone to pray while His disciples went into a boat to cross the sea. Jesus came to them by walking on the water! He fed 5,000 people and then He walked on water. In the Gospel of Matthew we see that He tested Peter's faith while He was walking on the water. He just tested Philip's faith before sundown, and then He tested Peter's faith that same night. The sea was rising due to the stormy weather and Jesus calmed the storm. After seeing these miracles, the Gospel of Matthew describes how the disciples in the boat swore, "Truly you are the Son of God."

Week 4: Flesh for Salvation

Day 3

Faith Alone

Read: John 6:22-47

Memorize/meditate: John 6:27

"Do not work for food that perishes but for the food that endures for eternal life, which the Son of Man will give you." (NABRE)

In this discourse Jesus stresses the necessity of believing in Him. He just performed miracles to emphasize their faith: fed 5,000, walked on water, calmed the storm and tested Philip and Peter's faith. Now He tells them to believe in Him in verses 29, 35, 36, 40, 47. That's 5 times in this reading that He stresses the necessity of their belief in Him. In verse 45 He makes reference to the prophecies of Isaiah 54:13 and Jeremiah 31:34 about the New Covenant. This is very important information regarding the New Covenant; God the Father brings us, His children, to Him through Jesus Christ in the

New Covenant. Notice that He even uses the double "Amen", which is a form of oath-swearing, 3 times in verses 26, 32, and 47, each time making a firm, but challenging statement to the crowd:

Verse 26: Amen, amen, I say to you, you are looking for me not because you saw signs but because you ate the loaves and were filled.

Verse 32: Amen, amen, I say to you, it was not Moses who gave the bread from heaven; my Father gives you the true bread from heaven.

Verse 47: Amen, amen, I say to you, whoever believes has eternal life.

Furthermore, He is urging them to believe because they are lacking faith. They just saw Him Feed the 5,000 people, yet they follow Him not because of the miracle He worked, but because of the fact that He fed them. They even ask for another sign so that they may believe. Jesus goes on to tell them in verse 44 and 46 that they will not be able to believe in Him unless the Father draws them, for "everyone who listens to my Father and learns from Him comes to me." Remember, the Father has spoken and said, "He is my Beloved Son . . . Listen to him." Now the Beloved Son swears, "Amen, amen, I say to you, whoever believes has eternal life (Jn 6:47)."

Week 4: Flesh for Salvation

Day 4

Bread of Life

Read: Exodus 16:11-15. 31, 35; John 6:30-33, 48-51

Memorize/meditate: John 6:51

"I am the living bread that came down from heaven, whoever eats this bread will live forever; and **the bread** that I will give **is my flesh** for the life of the world." (NABRE)

Look closely at this verse: the statement is an equation of truth:

the bread= my flesh

The bread that He will give for the life of the world is His flesh. He, in the flesh, was crucified and died on the cross; and in this reading, He says that the same **flesh** that He will sacrifice on the cross for us **is** the **bread** that He will give us to eat. He is giving a promise of a miracle superior to the miracle of the bread in the Old Covenant.

Let's look at the miracle of the manna from heaven. God performed the miracle of manna from heaven for the Israelites to survive in the desert for 40 years. This means several hundred tons of manna falling from the sky daily for 40 years. Jesus states that this miracle is *inferior* to the one that He will give for everlasting life. Jesus says in Jn 6:49-50, "You ancestors ate manna in the desert, but they died; this is the bread that comes down from heaven so that one may eat it and not die." So their ancestors ate the manna that fell from heaven and lived their earthly lives, but it did not gain them *everlasting* spiritual life, which Jesus is promising them now with His bread. He will give them the "true bread" from heaven which "gives life to the world."

It's noteworthy that He has been purposely emphasizing faith so strongly in this chapter, John 6, through miracles and through discourse, because the disciples need it in order to be obedient to His command. He fed 5,000 people bread which they physically ate; the Passover feast is near, which is a meal to be physically eaten; and He spoke about the bread that the ancestors in the desert physically ate. There are a lot of cues for eating so far in John chapter 6. Let's recap what Jesus said in this teaching: first, He said, "Do not work for the food that perishes but for the food that endures for eternal life (verse 27)", then He said, "My Father gives you the **true bread** from heaven . . . which . . . gives life to the world (verse 32-33)", then He said, "I am **the bread** of life (verse 35), then He said, "Amen, amen, I say to you, whoever believes has eternal life." Then He said, "I am **the bread** of life. Your ancestors ate the manna in the desert, but they died; this is **the bread** that comes down from heaven so that one may eat it and not die. I am **the living bread** that came down from heaven; whoever eats this **bread** will live forever; and **the bread** that I will give **is my flesh** for the life of the world (verses 48-51)." If our ancestors physically ate the manna which God the Father gave them in the desert, then we must also physically eat **the bread** which God the Son will give us; and **the bread** that He will give us **is His Flesh**.

Now let's remember what St. Paul told us was his job in passing on the teachings of Christ, ". . . to bring about the obedience of faith . . ." It is in our *obedience* to God's word that we live out our faith, and it is **faith alone** which gives us everlasting life."

Week 4: Flesh for Salvation

Day 5

Flesh to Eat?

Read: John 6:52-59

Memorize/meditate: John 6:54

"Whoever eats my flesh and drinks my blood has eternal life, and I will raise him on the last day." (NABRE)

The bread of life discourse caused quarreling amongst the Jews in verse 52: "How can this man give us his flesh to eat?" With all the cues of physical eating present—feeding 5,000, Passover near, manna in the desert, true bread from heaven—they are taking Jesus' words literally and not figuratively. How does Jesus respond to their quarreling? He *emphatically* states with a double "Amen", which is oath-swearing language, that they are to eat His flesh and drink His blood, "Amen, amen, I say to you, unless you **eat the flesh** of the Son of Man and drink his blood, you do not have life within you (verse 53)."

In fact, He is so serious in His oath that He repeats Himself 7 times in a row in verses 53-58, even swearing on His Father in heaven in verse 57, "Just as the living Father sent me and I have life because of the Father, so also the one who feeds on me will have life because of me." We should now ask ourselves, "Do I believe the Father sent Him? Do I believe that He has life because of the Father? Do I need to **eat His flesh**, which is true food?"

This is not the language of figurative or symbolic speech; rather, this is the language of solemnity and truth. He told us 5 times to believe in Him, verses 29, 35, 36, 40, 47 and He told us 8 times to **eat His flesh**, verses 50, 51, 53, 54, 55, 56, 57, 58 in this chapter. If we believe in Him then we **do whatever He tells us** to do; to be faithful to Him we must be obedient to Him.

Listen to Him:

Amen, amen, I say to you

Whoever believes has eternal life.

I am the bread of life.

Whoever **eats this bread**

Will live forever.

Week 4: Flesh for Salvation

Day 6

Too Hard to Accept

Read: John 6:60-71

Memorize/meditate: John 6:68

"Master, to whom shall we go? You have the words of everlasting life."
(NABRE)

In this reading we see that the disciples were murmuring, "This saying is hard; who can accept it?" The way that Jesus responded to their mumbling was to challenge their faith, "Does this shock you? What if you were to see the Son of Man ascending to where he was before?" He challenges them to believe in truth. It is true that He ascended to where He was before as it's recorded in the Gospel of Mark 16:19 ". . . Jesus . . . was taken up into heaven . . ." and in the Gospel of Luke 24:51 "As he blessed them he . . . was taken up to heaven."

So, if it is true that He would ascend to where He was before, then it is also true that He is the bread of life and whoever **eats this bread** will live forever.

The occurrence of this dialogue is happening one year before His death and the disciples are struggling to believe what he is talking about—Eat His Flesh? Ascend to where He was before? Nevertheless, He remains steadfast in His teaching that **He is the true bread** that has come down from heaven and the one that feeds on Him will have life because of Him. Some of the disciples could not accept this doctrine and they left Him and "returned to their former way of life and no longer accompanied him."(verse 66) Now Jesus had been in the public ministry for 2 years and some of these disciples had been following Him for these 2 years, but when they leave He does NOT CALL THEM BACK. Why? Because He knows that they understand the literal teaching for eating His flesh, but they cannot accept His doctrine for eternal life: that **one must eat** His Flesh and drink His Blood to have eternal life. He doesn't call them back and tell them that they misunderstood Him and that He was only speaking symbolically, because He *wasn't* speaking symbolically. They understood Him to be speaking literally about the subject and they could not accept it. He even challenged the Apostles after the unbelieving disciples left, "Do you also want to leave?" But notice that He does not *retract* the teaching that is so hard to accept—*too hard* for some to accept. Peter answers His challenge with conviction, "Master, to whom shall we go? You have the words of everlasting life. We have come **to believe** and are convinced that you are the Holy One of God. (verses 68-69)."

Amen, amen, I say to you,

Whoever Believes has eternal life.

I am the living bread

That came down from heaven;

Whoever **eats** this bread

will live forever**;**

and the bread that I will give

is **my flesh**

for the life of the world.

Week 4: Flesh for Salvation

Day 7

Eat My Flesh

Read: John chapter 6

Memorize/meditate: John 6:4

"The Jewish feast of Passover was near." (NABRE)

    As you read this chapter recall what the first Jewish feast of Passover celebrated: deliverance from death for the first-born of the Israelites. Notice the structure of this chapter: Jesus performed miracles to emphasize faith; He tested the faith of Philip; He taught about the importance of having faith in Him and believing in Him; He taught about eating His flesh for everlasting life; the unbelieving disciples left Him; and finally, He did not call the disciples back, but instead He challenged those who remained. The fact that the disciples left His teaching is *very* significant, as it is the *only time* recorded in the New

Testament that any of His disciples left Him because they could not accept His teaching.

Another point to make note of is that the reference to the New Covenant would be *inside* them; "I will place my law within them and write it on their hearts." (Jer 31:33) Jesus calls us to intimate union with Him in the doctrine of the New Covenant, "Whoever **eats my flesh** and drinks my blood remains in me and I in him."

The Israelites ate the flesh of the Passover lamb for deliverance of their first-born from natural death, but it did not bring about eternal salvation, which was lost through the sin of Adam; whereas, Jesus says that if we eat His flesh we will have eternal salvation. See the New Testament reality of the Old Testament symbol:

Eat the flesh of the lamb

For salvation of natural life.

Becomes

Eat the flesh of the Lamb

For salvation of spiritual life.

Homework

For

Week 4

1.)   Look at John 4:31-34 and Matthew 16:5-12. See how the audience misunderstands Jesus and how He clarifies Himself. Now look at these passages: John 3:3-6; 11:11-14; 8:21-23; 8:39-44; 16:18-22; and Matthew 19:24-26. In all of these passages the audience misunderstands Jesus to be speaking literally and they raise objections, how does Jesus answer their objections? Does He repeat Himself or does He explain that He is only speaking figuratively?

_____

_____

_____

2.)   Look at Matthew 9:2-6 and John 8:56-59, the audience understands Jesus to be speaking literally. Does Jesus confirm or reject their inclinations? How?

_____

_____

_____

3.)   Look at John 6:52-58. How does Jesus handle the objections of the Jews?

_____

_____

_____

4.)   Refer to John 6:51. What is the bread that Jesus will give for the life of the world?

_____

_____

_____

5.)   Refer to John 6:32-33. Did Moses give the true bread from heaven? Explain. What is the true bread from heaven? Explain.

_____

_____

_____

6.) Refer to John 6:66-67. Scripture says that "many" left Jesus. Did He call them back? Why? In His life on earth, did He thirst for souls? Explain His actions.

_____

_____

_____

7.) Refer to John 6:67. How do you personally answer Jesus' question, "Do you also want to leave?" Explain.

_____

_____

_____

Week 5

The Last Supper Delivers

Week 5: The Last Supper Delivers

Day 1

Blood of the New Covenant

Read: Exodus 24: 7-8; Matthew 26:26-28; Mark 14:22-24; Luke 22:19-20; John 19:34; 1Corinthians 11:23-26

Memorize/meditate: Matthew 26:26

". . . Jesus took bread, said the blessing, broke it, and giving it to his disciples said, 'Take and eat; this is my body.'" (NABRE)

What we see in all of these readings is the distribution of the flesh and blood of the sacrificial offerings of the Covenants, Old and New. Notice the similarities in the language: Moses "took the blood and sprinkled it on the people, saying, 'This is the blood of the covenant . . . (Ex 24:8)'"; Jesus gave them the cup, "saying, 'Drink from it, all of you, for this is my blood of the covenant . . . (Mt 26:27-28)'" In the Old Testament the Lord told Moses to sprinkle the blood of the covenant on the people, while in the New Testament the Lord told the people to drink the blood of the covenant. The language used in Mt 26:28 when Jesus said, ". . . this is my blood . . . which will be shed . . . for the forgiveness of sins" is the same type of language which is used throughout the Old Testament in a sacrificial offering for the forgiveness of sins.

When we go back to the Old Covenant and read about sacrificial offerings, especially in the book of Leviticus, there are precise instructions about how the sacrifices are to be made, and precise instructions for what the priest is supposed to do with the body and blood of the sacrificed animal. In fact there was *never* any sacrifice made in the Old Testament without deliberate instructions on what to do with the sacrificed body. Moses carried out instructions given to him by the Father, commanding the people to *eat* the flesh of the lamb and *sprinkle* the blood on the people; and Jesus carried out the instructions given to Him by the Father, to command the people to *eat* His flesh and *drink* His blood. In the Old Testament Moses offered a sacrificed lamb; In the New Testament Jesus offers Himself as the sacrificed Lamb.

The earliest Christian church is recorded in the New Testament, and describes how they carried out Jesus' command for the passing on of the provisions of the New Covenant. In 1Cor 11:23 St. Paul describes that he is *able* to offer the sacrifice of the Lamb by the rite of Sacred Tradition, because "I received from the Lord what I also handed on to you . . ." He is describing the passing on of Sacred Tradition just as the traditions were passed on through the priesthood of the Old Covenant.

In the New Testament this Passover supper is Jesus' last Passover *and* His last supper; this is the night before His death. His previous Passover, (John chapter 6) was filled with teachings and promises regarding His Flesh and Blood. Compare John 6:51 with Matthew 26:26:

. . . and the bread that I will give is my flesh

For the life of the world.

. . . Jesus took the bread . . . said,

"Take and eat; this is my body."

Notice also the similarity in language when He fed the 5,000 people and then when He fed His Apostles at His last supper. He performed a miracle on *both* occasions. John 6:11 and Matthew 26:26:

Jesus took the loaves, gave thanks,

And distributed them . . .

Jesus took the bread, said the blessing, broke it,

And giving it to his disciples . . .

Remember from Week 1: Day 1 of this study that God's word becomes what it declares. By His declaration,

The bread becomes His Body.

His declaration = reality

His declaration of the New Covenant is:

"Take and eat: **This is My Body.**"

Week 5: The Last Supper Delivers

Day 2

The Christian Passover

Read: Exodus 12:8, 46; John 6: 53-58; 1Corinthians 5: 7-8; 1Peter 1:18-19

Memorize/meditate: 1Corinthians 5:7b

"For our paschal lamb, Christ, has been sacrificed." (NABRE)

The Passover sacrifice set forth in the Old Testament requires that the sacrificed lamb be eaten. Jesus is the Lamb of the new Passover, and He commands that we eat the flesh of the lamb:

Amen, amen, I say to you, unless you eat the flesh of the Son of Man and drink His blood, you shall not have life within you. Whoever eats my flesh and drinks my blood has eternal life and I will raise him on the last day. For my flesh is true food, and my blood is true drink. Whoever eats my flesh and drinks my blood remains in me and I in him. Just as the living Father sent me and I have life because of the Father, so also the one who feeds on me will have life because of me. This is the bread that came down from heaven. Unlike your ancestors who ate and still died, whoever eats this bread will live forever. (Jn 6:53-58)

The Passover tradition of the Old Testament is a **symbol** for deliverance, and in order for the people of the covenant to be saved, they must eat the lamb of sacrifice. **It must be eaten**. The Passover of the New Testament is the **reality** of deliverance, and in order for the people of the covenant to be saved, they must eat the Lamb of sacrifice. **It must be eaten**.

Old Covenant:

Eat the lamb and

The Lord delivers their

first-born from death

New Covenant:

Eat the Lamb and

The Lord delivers us

To eternal, spiritual life.

Week 5: The Last Supper Delivers

Day 3

Lamb of God

Read: Psalm, 110:1; Matthew 26:29; Mark 14:25; Luke 22: 15-16; John 1:29; Revelation 19:6-9

Memorize/meditate: John 1:29b; Revelation 19:9

"Behold, the Lamb of God, who takes away the sins of the world. Blessed are they who have been called to the wedding feast of the Lamb." (NABRE)

Jesus tells His Apostles that He will partake in this Passover supper with them in the Kingdom of God. In the book of Revelation John sees a vision of heaven and in his vision he sees the wedding feast. The wedding feast is the celebration of Christ and His Bride, the Church. The Church is married to Jesus and through the marital union "the two shall become one flesh." (Mt 19:5) It is interesting to note that at the last Passover feast that Jesus celebrated with His Apostles on earth He gave them His flesh to eat and He promised to celebrate this feast with them again from heaven. Jesus is married to the Church and the two become one flesh; so the congregation of the Church in heaven and on earth is offered the one-flesh union with Jesus Christ. When the Apostles consumed his Flesh, they literally became one with Jesus. Jesus has made a perfect marriage in becoming one flesh with His Church, and the Body of Christ is offered eternally in heaven and on earth at the wedding feast of the Lamb.

Week 5: The Last Supper Delivers

Day 4

Once for All

Read: Psalm 110:1, 4; Hebrews 7:23-25; 9:24-26; 10:8-12

Memorize/meditate: Hebrews 7:24

". . . but He, because He remains forever has a priesthood that does not pass away." (NABRE)

The body of Jesus Christ is offered **once** for all because Jesus is an eternal being; His offering is an *eternal* offering. His office continues forever, it is an everlasting priesthood, so that He remains in office and continues to offer from heaven what is offered by Him on earth, His Body. In this manner of continuing His offering through an eternal sacrifice in heaven and on earth, He "marries" heavenly worship with earthly worship through His offered sacrifice, which is **once for all**. The Body of Christ is an eternal being so His offering occurs once in *eternity* not once in history.

The priesthood of the Old Testament offered sacrifices daily, each time offering a new sacrifice unto the Lord. Jesus offered His Body as a sacrifice, and He continues to offer His Body since His office of priesthood remains firm forever. The priests of the Old Testament died, but the high priest of the New Testament, Jesus Christ, lives eternally and offers eternally so **His priesthood does not pass away.**

Week 5: The Last Supper Delivers

Day 5

The Passover Lamb

Read: Exodus 12: 6, 22, 46; Luke 23: 52-54; John 19: 14-16, 29-30, 36

Memorize/meditate: Exodus 12:6b

"with the whole assembly of Israel present, it shall be slaughtered during the evening twilight." (NABRE)

There is an intensely direct correlation in Scripture between the Passover regulations and the sacrifice of Jesus. Jesus is a sacrificed Lamb, sacrificed for the forgiveness of our sin, but He is not *just a lamb*; He is our **Passover Lamb.** The Gospels record how Jesus purposefully made His way to Jerusalem for the Passover (see Matthew 21:1-11, Mark 11:1-11, Luke 19:28-40, John 12:12-19). Jesus was identifying Himself with a Passover lamb. He gave shocking testimony during the previous Passover in John 6, about how one would have to eat *His* Flesh to have life. In fact, close scrutiny of His last Passover supper with

His Apostles reveals an absence of the last glass of wine which was traditionally drunk during the celebratory meal. This last glass of wine is then offered to Jesus as He is dying on the cross, and what are His words after drinking from this cup? "It is finished (Jn 19:30)." He has finished the requirements for His Passover offering.

Recall that in the Old Testament the only sacrificial offering that was eaten as a memorial meal was the Passover sacrifice, and there was not one sacrifice offered without precise ritual specifications for the rendering of the sacrificed body. The sacrificial offerings are sacred and there are precise indications for the relinquishment of the sacrificed body. The Passover lamb was to be eaten as a meal by the Israelites; it was the only sacrifice that was eaten by a community of people.

This brings to mind some questions regarding the circumstances of Jesus' death: Why did He identify Himself so strongly with a *Passover sacrifice?* Why did the events of His death correspond, almost as if on cue, with the Jewish ceremony of the Passover sacrifice? Why did Jesus tell His disciples at the previous Passover that they would need to eat His Flesh and drink His Blood to have life within them, and why did He repeat Himself *six* times in a row (Jn 6:53-58)? Why did He say, "I am the bread of life . . . whoever eats this bread will live forever; and the bread that I will give is my flesh for the life of the world?" (Jn 6:48, 51) Why did He give His apostles *bread* at His last supper and bless it saying, "Take and eat; this is my *body* (Mt 26:26)"? Why did He die on the cross?

Week 5: The Last Supper Delivers

Day 6

Fulfillment of the Law

Read: Exodus 12:24-27; 1Peter 1:18-19; Revelation 5: 11-13; 19:7, 9

Memorize/meditate: Exodus 12:25

"Thus, you must also observe this rite when you have entered the land which the Lord will give you as He promised." (NABRE)

The Passover was a feast of perpetual ordinance as set down by the Lord in the Old Testament and it was to be observed again upon deliverance to the Promised Land: "Thus, you must also observe this rite . . ." (Ex 12:25) The Christian Passover is also a feast of perpetual ordinance as set down by the Lord in the New Testament: "Do this in memory of me." (Lk 22:19) Jesus commands His disciples to observe this offering in His stead. The celebration of the feast of the Christian Passover, the "wedding feast of the Lamb" (Rev 19:9), is the New Testament fulfillment of the Old Testament Law. It is a divine fulfillment of the Law, because the Lamb of God lives forever in heaven and "the wedding day of the Lamb has come" (Rev 19:7); the wedding day is an eternal event in heaven. The wedding feast, therefore, is an eternal event in heaven. The wedding feast, therefore, is an eternal banquet in heaven; because, the Lamb of God is forever.

In the Old Testament, the Lord commanded the Israelites to observe the Passover feast when they were delivered to the Promised Land. What is the Promised Land that Jesus delivers us to in the New Testament? He promises us eternal life with our Father in heaven if we eat His Flesh and drink His Blood. He is offering us a Passover meal that will deliver us into the eternal Kingdom of God; and once we get there we must also observe this Passover rite as foretold in the events of the Old Covenant. Jesus tells His disciples that He will celebrate the Passover meal with them again in heaven (Mt 26:29; Mk 14:25; Lk 22:15-16), Just as the Israelites would celebrate the Passover meal together again when they reached their promised land. At the eternal banquet in heaven God says, "Blessed are those who have been called to the wedding feast of the Lamb" (19:9). The symbol of the Old Testament gives rise to the reality of the New Testament:

Old:

Passover feast = deliverance to Promised Land

New:

Passover feast = deliverance to Kingdom of God

Week 5: The Last Supper Delivers

Day 7

Body and Blood

Read: Matthew 26:26-28; Mark 14: 22-24; Luke 22: 19-20; John 6: 53-58; 1Corinthians 10: 16-17; 11:28-29

Memorize/meditate: 1Corinthians 11:29

"For anyone who eats and drinks without discerning the body, eats and drinks judgment on himself." (NABRE)

Notice the pattern in these readings: Matthew, ". . . this is my body . . . this is my blood . . ."; Mark, ". . . this is my body . . . this is my blood . . ."; Luke, ". . . this is my body . . . this cup is the new covenant in my blood . . ."; John ". . . My flesh is true food and my blood true drink."; St. Paul "The cup . . . is it not . . . the blood of Christ? And the bread . . . is it not . . . the body of the Lord? For anyone who eats and drinks without discerning the body, eats and drinks judgment on himself." If we all partake in "the wedding feast of the

Lamb," that is, if we all eat the body of Christ and drink the blood of Christ then "we, though many, are one body." (1Cor 10:17) In the marriage of Christ to His Bride, the Church, "the two shall become one flesh; so they are no longer two, but one flesh." (Mt 19:5-6) We become united to the body of Christ through the one-flesh union of the wedding feast; thus, when we eat His flesh and drink His blood "we, though many, are one body" in Christ, our Lord.

Remember, the word of God creates what it declares;

IT IS POWERFUL:

Created the universe, created all life on earth

Gave sight to the blind, cast out demons

Multiplied bread, calmed the storm,

Healed the sick, raised the dead,

Turned the water into wine,

Turned the bread into

His flesh,

Turned

the

wine

into

His blood.

Homework

For

Week 5

1.) In the Aramaic language of Jesus' time, the figure of speech "to eat the "flesh" or "to drink the blood" of someone meant to persecute, assault and destroy them. See how the expression is used in Psalm 27:2; Isaiah 9:18-20, 49:26; Micah 3:3; 2Samuel 23:15-17; Revelation 16:6, 17:6, 16. When Jesus tells us to eat His Flesh and drink His Blood could He have been using the figurative expression meaning to persecute, assault, and destroy Him or is He speaking literally? What is He calling us to do?

_____

_____

_____

2.) What is Christ's relationship with the Church? Refer to Mt 9:15; Mk 2:19-20; Lk 5:34-35; Eph 5: 21-32; Rev 19: 7, 21:2, 9; 22:17.

_____

_____

_____

3.) What is God's definition of marriage? Refer to Gen 2:24; Mt 19:5; Mk 10:7-8; Eph 5: 31. What does this mean to you?

_____

_____

_____

4.) In a marriage between man and wife, there is an intimate, life-giving physical union which unites them as "one flesh". How do the members of the Church, the Bride of Christ, physically receive Christ, the Bridegroom, in an intimate, life-giving union? See John 6:56. How does He physically give Himself to Her in a life-giving way? See John 6:51.

_____

_____

_____

5.)   What is the powerful event that gives the opportunity for Jesus to physically unite Himself to His Bride? See Day 3 of this week's study.

_____

_____

_____

6.)   Which sacrifice of the Old Testament was eaten as a meal by the community? Refer to Exodus chapter 12.

_____

_____

_____

7.)   In the Old Testament, sacrifices are offered for sin and then the body of the sacrifice is considered sacred and must be burned according to the law (Lev 4:12, 4:21). The New Testament says that the Lamb of God is offered "once for all" (Heb 10:10). What happened to the body of the Lamb after He was sacrificed? See Luke 24:1-7. How does this affect us?

_____

_____

_____

Week 6

Back to the Word

Week 6: Back to the Word

Day 1

Teachings Handed Down

Read: Matthew 28: 18-20; 1Corinthians 11:2, 23-29, 15: 2-3

Memorize/meditate: 1Corinthians 11:23

"For I received from the Lord what I also handed on to you that the Lord Jesus, on the night he was handed over, took bread, and, after he had given thanks, broke it and said, "This is my body that is for you. Do this in remembrance of me." (NABRE)

Remember in the movie *Back to the Future*, when Michael J. Fox went back in time 30 years? He didn't know how to get back home, so he found Doc Brown, the inventor of the time machine that catapulted him back all those years, and he said to him, "I came here in a time machine *that you invented,* and I need *your help* to get back to the year 1985." Well, we also need to go back in time to the Apostles and the writers of the New Testament and say to them, "I'm reading the New Testament of the Holy Bible *which you wrote*, and I need *your help* to get me back to the future." The Bible will teach us how to follow Jesus, who is the Word and the Word is our past, present, and future, so we must go **back to the Word.**

As Christians we are *obligated* to go back to the early Christian Church and understand their faith and their doctrine. Why? Because the Word of God is eternal truth, which means that it is true *always*; the truth does not change even though our time and culture change. We need to understand that the Word of God is a person, Jesus Christ; He was made flesh and taught among us. He taught His disciples, they taught their disciples, they taught their disciples, and so on. His teaching was handed on from person to person. We must go back to the Early Church, because the Early Church was comprised of the Apostles and disciples who were teaching what they received from the Word Himself.

We have all probably discarded the directions for something in our lifetime, because we can "get by" without them, we don't really want to take the time to read all the detailed instructions when we can just "wing it". Do we want to "get by" on account of the teachings of Christ? Do we want the details? Do we really want to understand the fullness of faith that He taught?

If we want the fullness of the faith then we *must* follow the followers of Jesus. They not only received the full deposit of faith directly from Jesus, but they composed the New Testament, under the inspiration of the Holy Spirit; Jesus did not write down one word of His teachings, He gave the teachings orally, and He personally gave His disciples the authority to "hand on" what they learned from Him. As we read through the books of the New Testament, we can see the Church grow. We can see that the Church was living and teaching and passing on the faith even before the New Testament existed in writing. In fact the compilation of the New Testament was not even confirmed until about 400 years after Jesus' death, which means that the Church was living and passing on the faith of Jesus Christ by the authority and inspiration of the Holy Spirit which was given to her by Christ. Should we not go back to these early churches and see how they interpreted Jesus' teachings?

In Matthew 28:18, 20 Jesus states that He holds "all power in heaven and earth" and He personally commands His disciples to "observe all that I have commanded you." Who has all power in heaven and earth? Jesus does. And who does He command? He commands His disciples. They taught with the authority that was given to them by Jesus Himself, so what were they teaching?

In 1Corinthians 11:23-29 St. Paul makes it clear that he "received from the Lord" the command to celebrate the wedding feast of the lamb. St. Paul also makes it clear that he personally "handed on" what he "received from the

Lord"; therefore, the orders are being passed on from person to person as was begun by the person of Jesus Himself. The traditions of the Old Testament were also passed on from person to person in the Mosaic priesthood as begun by Moses.

As a priest Jesus blessed the bread and wine and declared it to be His body and blood, thereby *changing the substance* of the bread into His body and *changing the substance* of wine into His blood, which He offered as a sacrifice for sin. He then commissioned the Apostles as His first ordained priests by commanding them "Do this in remembrance of me." The early Christians recognized His use of the Aramaic word for "to do/ to make" as it was used in the Old Testament—especially in the book of Leviticus—as meaning: "to make an offering". In the Old Testament, the sacrificial wording in Hebrew was commonly written as "do/make this offering" or "do/make this sacrifice" and is especially present in the book of Leviticus when offering sacrifices for the ordination of priests when Moses established the priesthood. Jesus used the same sacrificial language when speaking to His Apostles in Aramaic; therefore, they **understood** that He was giving them the command to offer the sacrifice of His body and blood in His stead when He told them to "*Do this* in remembrance of me."

Jesus appoints the Apostles as the first priests, "but he, because he remains forever, has a priesthood that does not pass away." (Heb 7:24) This means that He appoints priests and they ordain priests under them, and they ordain priests under them, etc., but all of these priests in the order of Jesus are actually *under His living command* as the eternal high priest. In other words, the priest who is by the order of Christ blesses the bread and wine on the altar during the celebratory feast, but it is actually Jesus Himself, because He remains in office forever (Heb 7:23-24), who consecrates the bread and the wine. The priest who offers the sacrifice of the Lamb on the altar is under the command of the high priest, Jesus Christ, who sends forth the Holy Spirit to change the bread into His Body and the wine into His Blood. How can we know that this change has occurred when the elements of the bread and wine *appear* to be the same? It is by our obedience of faith that we know this to be true. It is by **faith alone.**

Back to the Word

The early Christians wrote the New Testament and taught the Christian faith just as they received it from Christ Himself. Does not the author of a book have more authority than the book itself? The early Christians composed the books of the New Testament, being inspired by the Holy Spirit, and handed on the interpretation of their writings through the teaching authority of the Church. In order that we can be obedient of faith to our Lord Jesus Christ, we *must* go "back to the Word." Back to the time and culture in which Jesus, the Word, was teaching. Let us take a closer look at some of the early Christian teachings:

St. Paul wrote his first letter to the Corinthian Christians from Ephesus around the year 56 A. D. This letter was compiled by the authority of the Church, along with many other letters Paul wrote, in an authoritative list of 73 inspired books proposed for the canon of the Bible in the year 382 A. D. The canon of the Bible was confirmed in the year 393 A. D. and then again in the year 397 A. D. by the Church councils; in 405 A.D. the 73-book canon of the Bible was approved by the head of the Church, St. Innocent I who closed the canon of the Bible at that time.

In his letter to the Corinthians St. Paul writes strong testimony for the handing on of the traditions set forth by Christ:

". . . hold fast to the traditions, just as I handed them on to you." 1Cor 11:2

"Now I am reminding you, brothers, of the gospel I preached to you, which you indeed received and in which you also stand. Through it you

are also being saved, if you hold fast to the word I preached to you . . ."
1Cor 15: 1-2

"For **I received from the Lord what I also handed on to you,** that the Lord Jesus, on the night he was handed over, took bread, and, after he had given thanks, broke it and said, 'This is my body that is for you. Do this in remembrance of me.' In the same way also the cup after supper saying, 'This cup is the new covenant in my blood. Do this, as often as you drink it, in remembrance of me.'" 1Cor 11:23-25

St. Paul gives harsh reproofs to Christians who do not recognize Christ's body and blood made present by the Holy Spirit through the prayer that was handed on to them by Christ:

"Therefore whoever eats the bread or drinks the cup of the Lord unworthily will have to **answer for the body and blood of the Lord.** A person should examine himself, and so eat the bread and drink the cup. For anyone who eats and drinks without discerning the body, **eats and drinks judgment on himself.**" 1Cor 11: 27-29

St. Justin Martyr is considered the greatest Christian apologist (defender of the faith) of the second century. Around the year 150 A.D. he wrote his famous *Apology* to the Emperor in Rome. In it he writes a detailed description of Christian worship including:

We call this food Eucharist; and no one is permitted to partake of it, except one who believes our teaching to be true . . . For not as common bread nor common drink do we receive these; but since Jesus Christ our Savior was made incarnate by the word of God and **had both flesh and blood for our salvation,** so too, as we have been taught, **the food** which has been made into the Eucharist by the Eucharistic prayer *set down by Him,* and by the change of which *our flesh and blood is nourished,* **is both the Flesh and the Blood of that incarnated Jesus.**[1]

St. Ignatius of Antioch was a disciple and co-worker of the Apostle John. Around the year 110 A.D. he wrote seven letters to various churches on his way to be martyred in Rome. In his letter to the Smyrnaeans, St. Ignatius denotes those who do not recognize the body and blood of Christ as heretics:

Take note of those who hold heterodox opinions on the grace of Jesus Christ which has come to us, and see how contrary their opinions are to the mind of God . . . They abstain from the Eucharist and from prayer, because they do not confess that the Eucharist is the **Flesh of our Savior Jesus Christ, Flesh which suffered for our sins** and which the Father, in His goodness, raised up again.[2]

---

[1]   *First Apology* 66, 20; Jurgens, Page 55, #128.

[2]   *Letter to the Smyrnaeans* 6, 2; Jurgens, page 25, #64.

In his letter to the Romans, St. Ignatius writes:

> I have no taste for corruptible food or for the pleasures of this life. I desire the **Bread of God**, which is the **Flesh of Jesus Christ**, who was of the seed of David; and for **drink** I desire **His Blood**, which is love incorruptible.[3]

---

[3]   *Letter to the Romans* 7, 3; Jurgens, page 22, #54a

Week 6: Back to the Word

Day 2

Built on a Rock

Read: Matthew 7:24-29, 16:18

Memorize/meditate: Matthew 16:18

"And I say to you, you are Peter, and upon this rock I will build my church, and the gates of Hell shall not prevail against it." (NABRE)

Jesus says that a wise man built his house on a rock and then He says that He will build His Church, His house, on a rock. The wise man built his house on a rock and the rain fell, the floods came, and the winds blew and beat against that house. But it did not collapse; "**it had been set solidly on a rock**." (Mt 7:25) Compare this teaching with His intent to build His own house, His Church, ". . . upon this rock I will build my church and the gates of Hell shall not prevail against it." (Mt 16:18) He is giving the message of solidarity in foundation and the promise of the transmission of truth against all persecution.

The persecution will come, the gates of Hell will beat against the house and try to destroy it, but they will not succeed, because He will **set it solidly on a rock.** He is giving the *promise* of the permanence of the transmission of the truth of His Gospel teaching, through the impermeability of His house, which He will build on a solid foundation, like the wise man.

This is more than a promise; He is making a divine declaration in His statement, and when He makes a declaration truth issues forth and it **becomes reality**:

Upon this rock, **I will build my church**

And

The gates of Hell **shall not prevail against it.**

Back to the Word

St. Irenaeus was the second bishop of Lyons from about 180-200A.D. St. Irenaeus is considered one of the greatest theologians of the immediate post-Apostolic period, and he studied under St. Polycarp who was a disciple of the Apostle John who stood at the foot of the cross when Jesus was crucified. In his work, *AGAINST HERESIES,* St. Irenaeus makes the following statement about Jesus' Church:

> But since it would be too long to enumerate in such a small volume as this the successions of all the Churches, we shall confound all those who , in whatever manner, whether through self-satisfaction or vainglory, or through blindness and wicked opinion, assemble other than where it is proper, by pointing out here the successions of the bishops of the greatest and most ancient Church known to all, founded and organized at Rome by the two most glorious Apostles, Peter and Paul, that Church which has the tradition and the faith which comes down to us after having been announced to men by the Apostles. **For with this Church, because of its superior origin, all Churches must agree, that is, all the faithful**

in the whole world; and it is in her that the faithful everywhere have maintained the **Apostolic tradition.**[4]

---

[4]   *AGAINST HERESIES* 3, 3, 2; Jurgens, page 90, #210.

Week 6: Back to the Word

Day 3

High Priest Forever

Read: Genesis 14:18-20; 2Chronicles 19:11; Psalm 110:4; Malachi 2:7; Hebrews 5:1-10

Memorize/meditate: Psalm 110:4

The Lord has sworn and he will not repent: "You are a priest forever, according to the order of Melchizedek." (NABRE)

The Lord has sworn that Jesus is the high priest of the New Covenant. We are all sons and daughters of the Lord through the New Covenant, which is mediated by Jesus Christ. Jesus is eternal, so His priesthood and His sacrificial offering are both eternal—that is they continue forever.

He is a priest forever by the order of Melchizedek, and Melchizedek is a priest of God Most High, to whom Abraham gave a tenth of everything. Melchizedek brought out bread and wine for an offering; Jesus, being a priest by the order of Melchizedek, also brought out bread and wine for an offering. Jesus performed a miracle, turning the bread into His Body and the wine into His Blood and offered *himself* as a sacrifice. Then He told His Apostles to *"Do this* (offer this) in remembrance of me." He commissioned them as priests by His order, the order of Melchizedek. Jesus continues to offer in heaven what was offered on earth, His body; and through His priests He continues to offer on earth what He is offering in heaven, His body. Since His body is an eternal sacrifice it continues to be made available to His Church through the authority of His priests, because they are under His living, continuous authority as high priest.

In the Old Testament, the priesthood was very organized, and the order of priests could be traced from one priest to the priest who ordained him to the priest who ordained him and so on. When God established His covenant with the nation of Israel, He provided for a living, continuing authority in the Mosaic priesthood. When Christ established the New Covenant for all people He also provided for a living, continuing authority in His Church. Jesus is the high priest forever and He gave His commandments to His disciples personally and they personally passed on what was given to them by Him. The priests that He ordained went on to ordain priests under them, as St. Paul said, "For I received from the Lord what I also handed on to you . . ." (1Cor 11:23) The Lord commanded them and ordained them and they passed on what they received from Him and it will continue to be passed on through the ages in accordance with the Scriptures that the Lord Jesus Christ said, "upon this **rock I will build my church** and the gates of Hell shall **not** prevail against it." (Mt 16:18)." He is a wise man who has built His house on a solid foundation and **it will not collapse**.

Week 6: Back to the Word

Day 4

Feed My Sheep

Read: Isaiah 22:19-22; Matthew 16:18-19; John 21:15-17

Memorize/meditate: Matthew 16:19

"I will give you the keys to the kingdom of heaven. Whatever you bind on earth shall be bound in heaven; and whatever you loose on earth shall be loosed in heaven." (NABRE)

Jesus tells Peter that He will give him the keys to the kingdom of heaven. Jesus knows scripture better than anyone and He is certainly aware of the passage in Isaiah in which the key of the House of David is passed on and gives great authority to the Prime Minister of the Kingdom of David, who is a father figure and whose office would continue as long as the Kingdom of David continued. Jesus is giving Peter the keys of the kingdom of heaven in the *very same* manner: "Whatever you bind on earth shall be bound in heaven;

and whatever you loose on earth shall be loosed in heaven." Jesus is obviously giving great authority to Peter; Jesus has all power in heaven and earth, and He is appointing Peter with a supreme authority on earth. Jesus knows that He will offer His body as a sacrifice and enter into the heavenly kingdom for all eternity, so, like a good shepherd He makes appointment of Peter as the acting shepherd of His Church here on earth in order that His Gospel is passed on through the living, continuing authority of His Church.

Jesus commands Peter to "feed" His sheep. As the shepherd of Jesus' Church, which will stand firm forever according to Christ's promise (Mt 16:18), Peter is given command to "feed" the flock. The Passover Lamb must be eaten by the Christians in order that they are delivered to the Promised Land—the Kingdom of God, and Jesus commands Peter with weighty importance, 3 times in a row. He also gives him the keys to the Kingdom of God and the power to bind and loose. Peter has been given the awesome responsibility to take charge of the Church of Christ and to feed all of the followers of Christ. Peter is therefore appointed by Jesus as the *Shepherd* and the Father (Is 22:21) of the house that Jesus built, His Church.

As Jesus leaves earth to take His eternal place at the right hand of the Father, He leaves Peter to carry on His establishment of the New Covenant on earth. When Peter enters into the heavenly kingdom, his office will be fulfilled by another shepherd and the keys to the Kingdom of Heaven will be passed on, and the Church will continue throughout the ages against assault, persecution, and defilement, because Jesus has declared His divine stamp of protection on her: "The gates of Hell shall not prevail against it." For the Church is the house that Jesus built **on a rock**, but realize that She is more than that: She is *His Love, His Wife, His Body,* **His Bride with whom He has become one flesh**, and just as He gave Himself over to death on the cross for Her, so too will He **always protect Her** from His eternal post as High Priest forever at the right hand of the Father.

Back to the Word

For the first 250 years of Christianity the Roman Emperors ruled through persecution to destroy the faith. In the first 200 years of Christianity, every successor to St. Peter but one was martyred.

Although a Roman Emperor's greatest fear was a rival to his own throne, the emperor Decius (249-251 A.D.) made the following remark after he had the bishop of Rome executed in 250 A.D.:

"I would far rather receive news of a rival to the throne than of another bishop of Rome."[5]

---

[5]   *CHRISTIAN HISTORY*, Issue 27 entitled "Persecution in the Early Church" (1990, Vol. IX, no. 3), page 22.

Week 6: Back to the Word

Day 5

Authority of the Holy Church

Read: Matthew 18:15-18; John 14:15-18; 21:25; Acts 2:42-47

Memorize/meditate: Matthew 18:17

"If he refuses to listen to them, tell the church. If he refuses to listen even to the church, then treat him as you would a Gentile or a tax collector." (NABRE)

Jesus speaks of the church as being the authority on *all* matters. He gave His disciples authority to bind and loose in His name, and He told them that He would bind in heaven what they bound on earth and He would loose in heaven what they loosed on earth. He implemented the hierarchy of His church: He is the high priest and the disciples are under His command; they are given the order to make disciples of all nations (Mt 28:19), and Jesus gave them specific orders to "Teach them to observe *all* that I have commanded you." (Mt 28:20) Not all of His teachings were committed to writing as John testifies in John

21:25 "There are also many other things that Jesus did, but if these were to be described individually, I do not think that the whole world would contain the books that would be written." Many of these teachings were handed on by what Christians call Sacred Tradition*, as St. Paul instructs : "So brethren, stand firm and hold to the traditions which you were taught by us, either by word of mouth or by letter (2Thess 2:15)."

Especially throughout the book of Acts we can see the Church growing from infancy. The disciples were to teach the Christian faith according to all the commands Jesus personally gave them, and we can see the devotions of the faithful as the apostles taught and passed on what they received from Christ, "and every day the Lord added to their number those who were being saved." (Acts 2:47)

Throughout the Old Testament God was extremely organized in all methods, and He continues to work within an organized framework in establishing the New Covenant. It is the desire of Christ that the Church fulfills her mission to pass on the truth in the fullness of His teachings and He intends to guide her in her mission. Jesus promised in John 14:15-18 that He would send the Holy Spirit to guide and safeguard the Church; He would not leave them

---

* Sacred Tradition—divine truth given to the Church by the oral testimony of Jesus or the Apostles under the inspiration of the Holy Spirit

orphans. In Mt 28:20, He promised "And behold, I am with you always." Christ will never leave His Church. He can't, **She is His Body**.

Back to the Word

St. Irenaeus, who was taught by St. Polycarp, who was a disciple of St. John the Apostle, who stood at the foot of Jesus' cross, is considered to be the greatest theologian of the immediate post-Apostolic period and in his work *AGAINST HERESIES* (180-199 A. D.), he testifies to the safeguard and transmission of the truth by the authority of the Church:

When, therefore, we have such proofs, it is not necessary to seek among others the truth which is easily obtained from the Church. For the Apostles, like a rich man in a bank, **deposited with her** most copiously **everything which pertains to the truth . . .**"[6]

---

[6] *AGAINST HERESIES* 3, 4, 1; Jurgens, p. 90, #213

Week 6: Back to the Word

Day 6

One Body

Read: John 17: 17-23; Romans 12: 4-5; 1Corinthians 10:17, 12:12-13; Ephesians 4:4-6, 15-16

Memorize/meditate: John 17:22

"And I have given them the glory you gave me, so that they may be one as we are one." (NABRE)

One God, One Lord, One Spirit, One Church, One Body, One Faith sent forth from the Lord Himself into the world, transmitted throughout time under the guidance of the Holy Spirit, the Lord, the giver of life, who proceeds from the Father and the Son. One shepherd guiding One Church united in One Faith under the living command of Jesus Christ, One risen Lord, the head of One Body.

The Holy Church of God has always been united in one faith under one shepherd and stands as one body in the world fulfilling all the commands set forth by Jesus Christ. The heart of this one body is the heart of Christ Himself made truly present on Her altar by the prayer that was handed on by our Lord and invokes the life-giving power of the Holy Spirit, as it was present in the early Church, as it has always been present throughout Her history, as it will always be present according to His words: "He who eats my flesh and drinks my blood abides in me and I in him. As the living Father sent me, and I have life because of the Father, so he who eats me will live because of me." (Jn 6:56-57) "Take and eat; this is my body." (Mt 26:26)

Back to the Word

St. Irenaeus, the greatest theologian of the immediate post-Apostolic period and the student of St. Polycarp, who was the disciple of St. John the Apostle, who laid his head on Jesus' breast, writes testimony to the unity of faith in the Church in his document AGAINST HERESIES (180-199 A.D.):

For the Church, *although dispersed throughout the whole world* even to the ends of the earth, has received from the Apostles and from their disciples **the faith in one God . . ."**[7]

---

[7]   *AGAINST HERESIES* 1, 10, 1: Jurgens, p. 19, #45.

Truth Amidst Trial

In 1456 Johannes Gutenberg developed the printing press, and the first book off the printing press was the Holy Gutenberg Bible. This invention of mass production allowed for the availability of the scriptures in people's own homes, which gave rise to the private interpretation of the Biblical texts, although contrary to Biblical teaching, "Know this first of all, that there is no prophecy of scripture that is a matter of personal interpretation" (2Pt 1:20), and unfortunately, it also allowed for the propagation of heresy, both of which were impossible without the technology of the printing press. It was then that the community of the faithful was able to have Bibles in their homes for personal study, and it was soon thereafter, in the year 1527, that the Protestant Reformation proposed and propagated the idea of using the Bible Alone to teach the Christian faith, without the interpretation and teaching authority of the Church; a proposition that was *impossible* for the first 1500 years of Christianity.

Since the introduction of the doctrine of using the Bible Alone for passing on the Christian faith, Christianity has dissented into over 28,000 (and counting!) different denominations all teaching a different set of Christian doctrine, yet all teaching from the Bible Alone. The Church is the author of the books of the Bible and has always maintained the necessity of an official interpreter. The books of the New Testament came forth from within the Church. Can we propose to interpret and teach a book *better* than its author?

In reaction to the Reformers, the Church assembled at the Council of Trent and addressed the issues brought to the forefront by the Reformers; one of the doctrines in question was the Real Presence of Christ on the altar, an issue which deals with the heart of the Church; therefore the council treated the subject exhaustively. One of the statements made by the Council was this:

> The Church of God has always believed that immediately after the consecration the true Body and Blood of our Lord, together with His soul and divinity, exists under the species of bread and wine. His Body exists under the species of bread and His Blood under the species of wine **according to the import of the words**.

St. Robert Bellarmine (1542-1621) was one of the greatest defenders of the Christian faith living in the period just after the dissent of the Church by the Protestant Reformation. St. Robert Bellarmine gives Biblical and historical citations for belief in the Real Presence of Christ on the altar:

TAKE AND EAT: THIS IS MY BODY. Weigh carefully, dear brethren, the force of those words. Surely laws and decrees ought to be promulgated in clear, precise, simple terms and not obscurely or ambiguously. Otherwise any man might plead ignorance and say, "Let the legislator speak plainly if he wants his law to be kept."

Now what Christian ever doubted that our Lord in instituting this Sacrament gave orders and framed a law that it was to be renewed perpetually in His church? "Do this," he said, "in memory of me." Since, then, these words of Christ are the expression of a law or command, to read figures and metaphors into them is to make Almighty God the most imprudent and incompetent of legislators. Again, a man's last will and testament should surely be drawn up in the straightforward speech of everyday life. No one but a madman, or one who desired to make trouble after his death, would employ metonymy and metaphor in such a document. When a testator says, "I leave my house to my son John" does anybody or will anybody ever understand his words to mean "I leave to my son John, not my house itself standing foursquare, but a nice painted picture of it?"

In the next place, suppose a Prince promised one of you a hundred gold pieces, and in fulfillment of his word sent a beautiful sketch of the coins, I wonder what you would think of his liberality? And suppose that when you complained, the donor said, "Sir, your astonishment is out of place, as the painted coins you received may very properly be considered true crowns by the figure of speech called metonymy," would not everybody feel that he was making fun of you and your picture?"

Now our Lord promised to give us his flesh for our food. "The bread which I shall give you," he said, "is my flesh for the life of the world." If you argue that the bread may be looked on as a figure of his flesh, you are arguing like the Prince and making a mockery of God's promises. A wonderful gift indeed that would be, in which Eternal Wisdom, Truth, Justice, and Goodness deceived us, its helpless pensioners, and turned our dearest hopes to derision.

That I may show you how just and righteous is the position we hold, let us suppose that the last day has come and that our doctrine of the Eucharist turns out to be false and absurd. Our Lord now asks us reproachfully: "Why did ye believe thus of my sacrament? Why did ye adore the host?" May we not safely answer him: "Yea, Lord, if we were wrong in this, it was you who deceived us. We heard your word, THIS IS MY BODY, and was it a crime for us to believe you? We were confirmed in our mistakes by a multitude of signs and wonders* which could have had you only for their author. Your Church with one voice cried out to us that we were right, and in believing as we did we but followed in the footsteps of all your saints and holy ones . . ."[8]

---

* For study on Eucharistic miracles, see Joan Carroll Cruz's excellent book, *Eucharistic Miracles* (Rockford, Illinois: TAN Books, 1987)

[8] James Brodrick, S. J., *Robert Bellarmine: Saint and Scholar* (Westminster, Maryland: Newman Press, 1961) pp 37-38

Week 6: Back to the Word

Day 7

Foundation of Truth

Read: 1Corinthians 10:14-17; 2Thessalonians 2:15, 3:6; 1Timothy 3:15-16

Memorize/meditate: 1Timothy 3:15

"But if I should be delayed, you should know how to behave in the household of God, which is the church of the living God, the pillar and foundation of truth."[9] (NABRE)

St. Paul gave instructions in his letter to Timothy making it clear that he intended to personally instruct him, but he wrote him the letter to have for guidance until his arrival. The Church was living already while the letters of St. Paul were in the process of being written, which is Biblical evidence that the Church was teaching the faith *before* the written documentation existed

---

[9]   Also for further study, see www.miraclerosarymission.org/lanciano.html www.
therealpresence.org/eucharist/mir/lanciano.html

which made up the New Testament of the Bible. Christ instituted His Church by saying, "upon this rock I will build my church, and the gates of Hell shall not prevail against it" (Mt 16:18); His statement promises that His Church *is founded on truth* and will be *sustained by truth*. St. Paul confirms that She is built on a rock for he calls Her "the pillar and foundation of truth." (1Tim 3:15) The truth was manifested in the flesh and it is on the Truth incarnate that the Church was founded and it is on the Truth incarnate that the Church is sustained.

St. Paul says about Christ in 1Tim 3:16, "Undeniably great is the mystery of devotion, who was manifested in the flesh . . ." and this same flesh is perpetually offered to us by Christ through the pillar and foundation of truth, His Church. All who partake in the bread and wine at the wedding feast of the Lamb, which is celebrated by His command, are participating in the body and blood of the Lord (1Cor 10:16); and in doing so, the hearts of the faithful become united with the Lord, and the Church remains one body unified under Christ who is the head of the body, just as He prayed at the Last Supper in John 17:20-21:

I pray not only for them, but also for those who will believe in me through their word. So that they may all be one, as you, Father, are in me and I in you, that they also may be in us, that the world may believe that you sent me.

Back to the Word

The traditions that were handed on by the Apostles as they were received from Christ included the authority to celebrate and participate in the wedding feast of the Lamb according to His command. All Early Christians remained united in faith of the Real Presence of Christ on the altar, as St. Cyril of Jerusalem states in 350 A.D.:

He himself, therefore, having declared and said of the Bread, "This is My Body," who will dare any longer to doubt? And when He Himself has affirmed and said, "This is My Blood," who can ever hesitate and say it is not his Blood?[10]

Do not, therefore, regard the bread and wine as simply that, for they are, **according to the Master's declaration**, the Body and Blood of Christ. Even though the senses suggest to you the other, **let faith make you firm**. Do not judge in this matter by taste, but be fully assured by faith, not doubting that you have been deemed worthy of the Body and Blood of Christ.[11]

For the early Christians, this doctrine must have been difficult for some of them to accept, and they were living and teaching the faith in the time of the

---

[10]   Catechetical Lectures: 22 (Mystagogic 4), 1; Jurgens, p 360, #843.

[11]   Catechetical Lectures: 22 (Mystagogic 4), 6; Jurgens, p 361, #846

Apostles and their disciples. In our day we have neither the Apostles nor direct disciples of them, and so we are called to an even deeper faith in accepting this doctrine as true. As St. Cyril asserts, "Even though the senses suggest to you the other, let faith make you firm." It takes **obedience of faith** to know the Real Presence of Christ our Lord on the altar in the form of bread and wine. It takes **Faith Alone** to know that His eternal body, which is truth incarnate, is made present in the living sacrifice on the altar of His Church by the command that was handed down by Him and which invokes the power of the Holy Spirit, the Lord, the Giver of Life, who proceeds from the Father and the Son to give life to the world.

A Miracle of the Heart

Around 700 A. D. a priest in a monastery in Lanciano, Italy had serious doubts about the Real Presence of Christ on the altar. During the Holy Sacrifice of the Mass, after he said the words of consecration, the host was changed into a circle of live Flesh and the wine was changed into live Blood, which coagulated into five irregular globules. The priest realized that God had just visibly answered his doubts. The congregation was amazed and the Flesh and

Blood was put on permanent display in the church while news quickly spread about town.

The miraculous Flesh and Blood have been examined over the centuries without any signs of fraudulence. In November 1970, a thorough investigation was begun which concluded in March 1971. The investigation was undertaken by the Italian Dr. Odoardo Linoli, Chief Physician of the "Ospedali Riuniti" of Arezzo and assisted by Dr. RuggeroBertelli of the University of Siena. The analyses yielded the following conclusions:

- The Flesh is real Flesh. The Blood is real Blood.

- The Flesh and Blood belong to the Human species.

- The Flesh consists of the muscular tissue of the heart.

- In the Flesh there is present in section: myocardium, endocardium, vagus nerve, and also the left ventricle of the heart for the large thickness of the myocardium.

- The Flesh is a "HEART" complete in its essential structure.

- The Flesh and Blood have the same blood-type; AB (Blood-type identical to that which Professor Baima Bollone uncovered in the Holy Shroud of Turin.)

- In the Blood there were found proteins in the same normal proportions as are found in the sero-proteic make-up of fresh normal blood.

- In the Blood there were also found these minerals: chlorides, phosphorous, magnesium, potassium, sodium, and calcium (normally found in blood).

- The preservation of the Flesh and Blood, which were left exposed to the action of atmospheric and biologic agents, remains an extraordinary phenomenon.[12]

---

[12] For further studies on this Eucharistic Miracle and others, see Joan Carroll Cruz's book, *Eucharistic Miracles* (Rockford, Illinois: TAN books, 1987)

Homework

For

Week 6

1.)   Write dictionary definitions for the following word:

appoint-

_____

_____

canon-

_____

_____

catholic-

_____

_____

commission-

_____

_____

dissent-

_____

_____

foundation-

_____

_____

heresy-

_____

_____

heterodox-

_____

_____

metonymy-

_____

_____

metaphor-

_____

_____

pillar-

_____

_____

propagate-

_____

_____

protestant-

_____

_____

universal-

_____

_____

2.)   Refer to John 20: 1-23. Jesus prayed for His Church to be united in faith as one body. Do you also pray for unity in the Christian faith? Give examples. Read Matthew 12:30.

_____

_____

_____

3.)   Read the Parable of the Sower in Matthew 13:1-9 and Jesus' explanation

for the parable in Matthew 13:18-23. How does this apply to His Apostles

and His Church?

_____

_____

_____

4.)   Read Matthew 16: 13-20. Jesus founded his Church on a rock, Peter.

Trace the pastors of your church back to the founder. Who is the founder

of your church and in what year was it founded? Which Christian church

can you trace back to Jesus? (Hint: Jesus gave Peter the keys to the

kingdom of heaven and a list of the successors to St. Peter can be found

online or at any public library.)

_____

_____

_____

5.)   Give Biblical explanations for the four marks of Jesus' Church:

1.   **One** (refer to readings for Week 6, Day 6)-

_____

_____

2.   **Holy** (refer to readings for Week 6, Day 5)-

_____

_____

3.)   **Universal** (refer to readings for Week 3, Day 3)-

_____

_____

4.)   **Apostolic** (refer to readings for Week 6, Day 1 and Day2)-

_____

_____

6.)   Is obedience of faith in Jesus' Church important or is His Church outdated in our present time and culture? Remember God's Word is eternal. Refer to Week 6, Day 1.

_____

_____

_____

7.)   What is the heart of Jesus' Church? Refer to Week 6, Day 6; Read "A Miracle of the Heart".

_____

_____

_____

Week 7

The Sacrifice of the Lamb

Week 7: The Sacrifice of the Lamb

Day 1

Love the Lord

Supplemental study (very important!): Watch the movie, *The Passion of the Christ*, one day this week.

Read: Deuteronomy 6:4-7; Matthew 22: 34-38; Mark 12: 28-30; John 14: 15, 21

Memorize/meditate: Mark 12:30

"You shall love the Lord, your God, with all your heart, with all your soul, with all your mind, and with all your strength." (NABRE)

Jesus calls us to love God first: "Love the Lord, your God, with all your heart, with all your soul, and with all your mind. This is the greatest and the first commandment." (Mt 22: 37-38) How do we live out our love for God? Jesus tells us, "If you love me, you will keep my commandments." (Jn 14:15) If we love Him with all our heart then obedience follows naturally. Just as we are obedient to our fathers on earth out of love for them, we are also called to be obedient to our Father in heaven out of love for Him. Obedience of faith is the reflection of love.

The Sacrifice of the Lamb

In the movie watch the love of the Son, the Lamb of God, for the Father through His obedient sacrifice as He offers Himself to bear the curses that were wrought by Adam's disobedience. (Gen 3: 17-19)

While you are watching the movie, listen to the spoken language which is Aramaic. What does Jesus and everyone else call Peter? They call him Cephas. The name Cephas means rock. Remember in Matthew 16:18 Jesus said, "You are Cephas, and upon this cephas I will build my church . . ." Jesus knew Cephas's faith, and He trusted in Cephas's faith in order to give him the keys to the kingdom of heaven and the authority to bind and loose in His name. As Christians we are called to be obedient of faith under the authority of Cephas, because Cephas is under the command of Christ.

Jesus is obedient to the Father because He loves Him with all His heart. He surrenders His will to the Father obediently in all things, even unto death. Let us pray that we also learn obedience of faith; that we may surrender our hearts under the authority of the Father in heaven from Whom all good things come.

Week 7: The Sacrifice of the Lamb

Day 2

Love One Another

Read: Leviticus 19:18; Matthew 5: 43-44; 22: 37-40; Luke 10: 36-37; John 13: 34; 15: 12-14

Memorize/meditate: John 15: 12-13

"This is my commandment: love one another as I love you. No one has greater love than this, to lay down one's life for one's friends." (NABRE)

Jesus calls us to great love. Love the Father first and foremost and secondly, love our neighbor. These two commandments are necessary, for "the whole law and prophets depend on these two commandments." (Mt 22:40) We must learn to love the Lord with all our heart and we must learn to love our friends with great mercy and forgiveness. Jesus has the heart of God, a heart full of love, and in loving obedience to the Father He sacrificed Himself for His friends. No one has greater love than this.

The Sacrifice of the Lamb

Watch the sacrifice of the Lamb in the movie. See how He lays down His life for us. This is how much He loves His friends, us. *We* are His friends if we keep His commands. (Jn 14:21, 15:14)

Week 7: The Sacrifice of the Lamb

Day 3

The Agony in the Garden

Read: Matthew 5: 44; 6:10; 26: 36-39; Luke 22: 42-44

Memorize/meditate: Luke 22: 42

"Father, if you are willing, take this cup away from me; still, not my will but yours be done." (NABRE)

Jesus taught us how to love and how to pray and how to live. He loved the Father above all things. He lived His life as a prayer that His will would be united with the Father in heaven, and He loved others as He loved the Father.

The Sacrifice of the Lamb

In *The Passion of the Christ* see His agony in the garden. He agonized so badly that His sweat became drops of blood from the bursting capillaries in

His head. Is it possible that He was agonizing about the souls that He had not yet won and He was now out of time? He told Peter, Cephas, and the others, "My soul is sorrowful, even to death." Watch as He approached Cephas and the others after agonizing in the garden. They had fallen asleep, and He said to them, "Cephas, you could not keep watch with me for one hour?" He withdrew from His disciples and prayed 3 times, each time they fell asleep upon his departure. He recognized that the human effort fell down on the job, "The spirit is willing, but the flesh is weak." (Mt 26:41); and He was deeply saddened that His time had come to leave them on their own.

He lived His life fishing for souls, and He continued to pray for others, enemies and persecutors included, even unto His death. He showed extraordinary compassion and mercy for human souls during His lifetime. He loved the Father with all His heart and He loved us as He loved the Father, and He deeply desired to lead us to His kingdom.

Watch His determination to carry out His Father's will, knowing that He still thirsts desperately to gain more souls in His kingdom, and His agony in the garden is tremendous over the loss of opportunity to minister to more souls. There is no voice from heaven booming through the clouds this time; however, the stillness of the night and the distraction from the master of deceit do not let Him doubt the presence and protection of the Father. Evil is present, but so is His Father.

Week 7: The Sacrifice of the Lamb

Day 4

The Scourging at the Pillar

Read: Matthew 6: 13; 27: 21-26; Luke 23: 18-25; John 19:1

Memorize/meditate: John 19:1

"Then Pilate took Jesus and had him scourged." (NABRE)

Pilate did not find fault with Jesus, but he would not go against the crowd for fear of a rebellion. He even washed his hands of the crime against Jesus. We must be careful not to repeat his actions in society. Every time we fail to stand up for what is right we are like Pilate who washed his hands of guilt, and if we are in a position of authority then we are called to the duty of foreseeing righteousness for our brothers and sisters.

The Sacrifice of the Lamb

Watch the horror of a scourging in ancient times and marvel at the life that Jesus had in Him after it was finished. This is a miracle.

The soldiers used braided leather thongs with metal balls woven into them to scourge Jesus. These ancient Roman floggings were deadly. The forceful attack of the instrument caused deep bruises and contusions in the flesh, which would burst open upon subsequent lashings. The weapon also had sharp pieces of bone and metal claws on it which would pierce and gouge the flesh. The back of a scourged victim was often laid open from the lacerations and abrasions so that the spine was exposed, radiating intense neuronal (nerve) pain throughout the body. After the epidermal, or surface layer, of the skin was withered away in the first few lashings the continuing onslaught of the torturous blows would tear into the sinews of the muscles and expose tendons, bowels, spine, and blood vessels, very often causing death or physiological shock from blood loss.

Watch how Jesus receives the suffering inflicted upon Him as He continues to wage the spiritual war during the trauma. Evil is present, but so is His mother.

Week 7: The Sacrifice of the Lamb

Day 5

The Crowning with Thorns

Read: Matthew 6: 12; 27: 27-31; Mark 15: 16-20; Luke 6:29

Memorize/meditate: Matthew 27: 28-29a

"They stripped off his clothes and threw a scarlet military cloak about him. Weaving a crown out of thorns, they placed it on his head, and a reed in his right hand." (NABRE)

Jesus taught us to forgive others and to allow God's will to be done on earth. He lived what he taught. He gave Himself freely and entirely for the sacrifice and he was an open vessel receiving and allowing for God's will to be done on earth through His body. Noticeably, through it all He was forgiving of those who trespassed against Him. Let us not forget His command to "love one another as I have loved you."

The Sacrifice of the Lamb

Watch how Jesus allows Himself to be given over to the Roman soldiers for torture and mockery. They place a crown of thorns on His head which scraped against His skull applying pressure and piercing pain to: the Cranial Nerves in the occipital area; the sensitive bony prominences of the temporal bones on each side of the skull above the ears; and along the left and right frontal eminences on the forehead and supra-orbital ridges directly over the eyes. It was a skull-crushing ring of stabbing pain and ceaseless pressure enclosing His cranium. They stripped off His clothes pulling at the open wounds and torn flesh, and put a scarlet cloak on Him. Then they bowed down before Him in mockery.

Adam's sin of disobedience brought about the curse "Thorns and thistles shall it bring forth to you." (Gen 3:18) Jesus bore the curse obediently in establishing the New Covenant.

We see all the Lamb's intense suffering as the New Covenant unfolds to envelop all mankind. Since it was necessary that the Lamb should suffer to save our souls, we should meditate on these sufferings; because it is through these sufferings of Christ that we are cleansed. It is our participation in His sufferings which cleanses our hearts, strengthens our will against temptation, deepens our trust in God, reduces our occasion to sin, allows us to find truth amidst trial, provides mortification (the decrease of self and increase of Christ), and results in the obedience of faith necessary to show the Father our love.

Week 7: The Sacrifice of the Lamb

Day 6

The Carrying of the Cross

Read: Matthew 6:9; 27: 32; Mark 8: 34-36; 15:21; John 14:6; 19:17

Memorize/meditate: Matthew 27:32

"As they were going out, they met a Cyrenian named Simon; this man they pressed into service to carry his cross."(NABRE)

Jesus is the Way to the Father, and if we want to come to Him then we must take up our cross and follow the way of the truth. We must follow the truth and be faithful to the truth, because the truth will not change and the truth will not go away, the truth is eternal, the Truth is Jesus Christ; and Jesus Christ is the Way and the Life. We must embrace the cross and stand firm in the truth amidst persecution, and we must defend the truth against all heresy out of love and honor for our God if we aim to hallow His name.

The way to the truth is through His Bride; the Bride will take us to Her Bridegroom. She has been standing firm in the transmission of truth for over 2000 years, and we must be obedient of faith to the truths that She hands on from generation to generation. Living in truth is living the way of the cross.

The Sacrifice of the Lamb

Jesus has all power in heaven and earth, and He could have easily escaped His capture and torture at any given moment, but He did not. He lived in honor and reverence for the Father, hallowing His name and surrendering His entire being to the plan and will of the Father. If it was in the Father's plan that the Lamb should suffer like this before death, we must not overlook it. We should be meditating on the passion Jesus endured for us.

Watch Jesus struggle on the way while carrying the cross. Jesus had lost so much blood from the scourging that he was in a physiological state of hypovolemic shock, that is, He had lost too much blood volume, and all of His organs were compensating for the loss. In a state of hypovolemic shock the body undergoes the following physiological compensations: the kidneys stop producing urine to save volume in the blood, the body is in a hyper state of thirst to replace volume, the heart beats harder and more rapidly as there is not enough blood in the chambers to pump efficiently, and the blood pressure drops dangerously low causing fainting or loss of consciousness. Jesus could not physically continue; it is no wonder that Simon of Cyrene was imported to help Jesus carry His cross.

Are we carrying our crosses and helping our brothers and sisters to carry their crosses as Jesus commanded us? "Love one another." (Jn 13:34) Every time we help others to be obedient of faith and follow the teaching of the Church, then we are like Simon of Cyrene helping them to live in the truth, the way of the cross.

Week 7: The Sacrifice of the Lamb

Day 7

The Crucifixion:
To Seven Himself

Read: Genesis 2: 16-17; 3:6; Matthew 6:11; 26: 26-28; 27:50-53; Luke 23:46; John 19:34

Memorize/meditate: Luke 23: 46

"Jesus cried out in a loud voice, 'Father, into your hands I commend my spirit'; and when he had said this he breathed his last." (NABRE)

Jesus died on the cross and the veil of the Temple was torn in two, which means that the New Covenant has been born by His death. Adam introduced sin into the world, and Jesus introduced life into the world. Adam took a horizontal position and honored himself instead of honoring God's command which came from above. Jesus took a vertical position, receiving the command from above and honoring the Father's plan from beginning to end. A horizontal line and a vertical line make a cross, on which Jesus made a perfect sacrifice. He surrendered Himself willingly and completely in order that we would have eternal life through the New Covenant. "For just as in Adam all die, so too in Christ shall all be brought to life." (1Cor15:22)

It is essential that we understand what a covenant is before we can know how to live in a covenant. A covenant is an unbreakable family bond that is created by the swearing of an oath. An oath is a promise that is sworn by the highest name, the name of God. If an oath is broken the curses of God's word would ensue. If an oath is kept the rewards of God's word are reaped. In the Hebrew language oaths were sworn by using a formula that translates into English as "I seven myself." People living in Jesus' time would have recognized this oath-swearing formula. We must research to find the meaning of covenant bonds and oath-swearing formulas as they understood them. The only way we can live in the New Covenant is to understand and **know the New Covenant**.

Jesus established the New Covenant by swearing an oath which He did by dying on the cross to "seven Himself" with all human souls. The earliest Christians recognized seven powers of the Spirit that issued forth from His body in His sacrificial death on the cross: baptism, confirmation, Holy Eucharist, reconciliation, holy matrimony, holy orders, and anointing of the sick. They recognized that when the powerful sevenfold gifts of the Spirit were received by people on earth, the people were united in a covenant bond with God through the Spirit: "It is the spirit that gives life, while the flesh is of no avail." (Jn 6:63) When we receive the powers of the Holy Spirit, we receive grace, truth, and love; we receive God—the Father, Son, and Holy Spirit, and through this covenant bond we become family with God, sons and daughters of the Father, brothers and sisters through Christ, united in love by the Holy Spirit.

Jesus' Church still recognizes seven powers of the Holy Spirit which came forth from His body and unite us to our Lord in the bond of the New Covenant: baptism, confirmation, Holy Eucharist, reconciliation, holy matrimony, holy orders, and anointing of the sick. These gifts came forth from Jesus' body when He died on the cross and they cannot be changed or revoked. His sworn covenantal oath is eternal; the New Covenant is everlasting. It is imperative that we recognize and understand the sevenfold properties of Jesus' suffering and death on the cross as a sworn oath, because a covenant does not exist without a sworn oath; and it is these seven powers that sanctify us and allow us to live as He beckons us, "Sanctify yourselves, then, and be holy; for I, the Lord, your God, am holy." (Lev 20:7; 1Pet1:16)

The birth of the Church was recognized by early Christians when, upon his death, "one soldier thrust his lance into his side, and immediately blood and water flowed out." (Jn 19:34) Jesus' body poured forth the gifts of the sacraments and the oath was sworn and the Church was born from His side, as Adam's bride was also born from his side.

The testimony of John 1:1-5, 14 for the birth of Jesus says:

In the beginning was the Word,

And the Word was with God,

And the word was God.

He was in the beginning with God.

All things came to be through Him,

and without Him nothing came to be.

What came to be through Him

Was life

And this life was the light

of the human race;

the light shines in the darkness,

and the darkness has not overcome it.

And the Word became flesh

And made His dwelling among us,

And we saw

His glory,

The glory as of the Father's only Son,

Full of grace and truth.

We could also say that the testimony for the birth of the Church is:

In the beginning was the Church,

And the Church was with Christ,

and the Church was Christ.

She was in the beginning with Christ.

All priests came to be through Her,

And without Her no priest came to be.

What came to be through Her priests

Was consecrated bread

And this bread gives life to the world.

This Truth continues to give life

And the gates of Hell

Shall not prevail against Her.

And the bread becomes Flesh

And nourishes us from within,

And we see His glory,

The glory as of only Christ's

True Flesh,

Full of grace and truth.

The Sacrifice of the Lamb

Watch the grueling crucifixion in *The Passion of the Christ*. When Jesus came to the top of the hill to be crucified He came face to face with Caiaphas, the high priest of the Temple. Jesus is taking his place as high priest, and He will be high priest forever, because He has a kingdom that does not pass away. At this moment of eye contact between Jesus and Caiaphas, we see the memory of Jesus teaching his disciples, "I am the good shepherd—I lay my life down for my sheep . . . This command is from my Father . . . There is no greater love than for a man to lay down his life for his friends . . . My commandment to you after I am gone is this: love one another as I have loved you; so love one another." Jesus is the high priest of the New Covenant and He offers His divine, unblemished self as a sacrifice, which the high priest of the Old Covenant could not offer.

The sacrifice of the Lamb is not a slaughter as in the Old Covenant animal sacrifices; rather, death by crucifixion is slow, torturous death by suffocation. Watch the horrifying physiological aspects of a crucifixion: one hand is nailed to the horizontal beam, severing or crushing the nerve in the hand, which would send excruciating pain down the arm; the other arm is stretched approximately six inches, which causes the shoulders to dislocate, and then it is nailed to the opposite side of the horizontal beam, again crushing or severing the nerve; the feet are nailed to the vertical beam, sending extraordinary pain signals along the nerve pathways of the legs, and a pedestal is pushed up under them; the cross is raised upright and the victim hangs helplessly as gravity pulls down on the dislocated torso; the diaphragm and accessory muscles in the chest are weighted by gravity which causes an inability to exhale as the chest is fixed in the inhaled position; the pedestal under the feet serves as a standing block so that the victim can push up against gravity in order to exhale; carbon dioxide builds up in the blood as the victim is unable to exhale sufficiently and gas exchange in the lungs slows down; respiratory acidosis occurs, causing the blood to become flooded with carbonic acid; the acidic predisposition of the blood gives rise to cardiac irregularity, resulting eventually in cardiac arrest.

As He goes to His death, we are reminded of what the sacrifice of His body is for us: **it is our daily Bread**. Jesus said, "I am the bread of life (Jn 6:35) and the **bread** that I will give is my **flesh** for the life of the world"(Jn 6:51); and then at His last supper He consecrated **bread** and gave it to His Apostles saying, "Take this and eat it; **this is my body which will be given for you.**" (Mt 26:26;Lk 22:19) Watch how His body is given for you on the cross. Through His mercy and love, He left us His body as our daily bread so that "whoever **eats this bread** will live forever." (Jn 6:51)

In His death on the cross, the sacrifice that He endured to give us our daily bread, watch how His mother, His Apostle John, and His disciple Mary look on in reverence at their Lord as He lays down His life of His own accord for them. You see that they are not merely watching in horror at the catastrophic events that are unfolding before their eyes, but they continue to follow Him reverently in worship and loving adoration. We should respond with this same reverence and adoration before our daily bread, for the consecrated bread **is His body which was given for us,** the Flesh which suffered and died for our sins.

The early Christians called this bread *Eucaristein*, which is Greek for "thanksgiving". We should remain in a constant state of thanksgiving for the sacrifice of the Lamb, for the Heart of the matter really is **Eucaristein**.

Homework

For

Week 7

1.)   Write the dictionary definition for the following words:

cohort-

_____

_____

communion-

_____

_____

covenant-

_____

_____

Eucharist-

_____

_____

hypovolemia (see *hypo*—+ *volume* +—*emia)*-

_____

_____

oath-

_____

_____

praetorium-

_____

_____

Pharisee-

_____

_____

Sacrament-

_____

_____

Saducee-

_____

_____

Sanhedrin-

_____

_____

scribe-

_____

_____

suffocate-

_____

_____

swear-

_____

_____

union-

_____

_____

2.) Skim through the book of Leviticus. Did any animal suffer upon sacrifice? Why does the Lamb of the New Covenant suffer?

_____

_____

_____

3.) See Luke 5:17; 6:19; 8:46; John 19:34. What seven sacraments did the early Christians recognize as powers that came forth from Jesus' body when His side was lanced open upon the cross? Refer to Day 7. How did a Hebrew in ancient Biblical times swear an oath? Refer to Week 7 Day 7 and Week 1 Day 2. Do we swear oaths in our present day?

_____

_____

_____

4.) What does the word *cephas* mean in Aramaic? Refer to Week 7 Day 1.

_____

_____

_____

5.) Skim through the book of Revelation. Jesus is recurrently referred to by the title of "Lamb". How many times does this title appear? What is the significance of the title?

_____

_____

_____

6.)   Reflect on John 1:29 and 1Corinthians 10: 16-17; 11:27-29. In St. Paul's day the term "answer for the body and blood" meant a sin of bloodshed or murder against a person. How does this fit into the context of these passages?

_____

_____

_____

7.)   Read "The Appearance on the Road to Emmaus" in Luke 24:13-35. How far were they travelling from Jerusalem to Emmaus? The disciples recognized Christ their Lord in Eucaristein. When were their eyes opened?

_____

_____

_____

Prepare to Receive

If you are prepared to explore the gift of receiving our Lord and Savior in the Sacrament of the Most Holy Eucharist then you should begin with prayer. Research the faith of the One, Holy, Universal/Catholic, and Apostolic Church by reading the Catechism of the Catholic Church, the Didache, and other Church documents which can be browsed in an online library at www.salvationhistory.com or www.vatican.com. Approach a priest at His Church for consultation. This would be a priest by the order of Peter, who was ordained by Jesus Christ, who is the high priest forever according to the order of Melchizedek, priest of God Most High. Go to His Church, His Bride; She is waiting for you and She will read to you the scriptures according to the content and unity of God's saving plan in Salvation History. She needs you in order to become one body in Christ our Lord.

References

James Brodrick, S. J., *ROBERT BELLARMINE: SAINT AND SCHOLAR* (Westminster, Maryland: Newman Press, 1961) pages 37-38.

Father Frank Chacon and Jim Burnham, *BEGINNING APOLOGETICS 1: HOW TO EXPLAIN AND DEFEND THE CATHOLIC FAITH (*San Juan Catholic Seminars[P.O. Box 5253, Farmington, NM, 87499-5253], 1993-1998).

Father Frank Chacon and Jim Burnham, *BEGINNING APLOGETICS 3: HOW TO EXPLAIN AND DEFEND THE REAL PRESENCE OF CHRIST IN THE EUCHARIST* (San Juan Catholic Seminars [P.O. box 5253, Farmington, NM, 87499-5253], 1999).

Father Frank Chacon and Jim Burnham, *BEGINNING APOLOGETICS II: HOW TO ANSWER JEHOVAH'S WITNESSES AND MORMONS* (San Juan Catholic Seminars [P.O. Box 5253, Farmington, NM, 87499-5253], 1996).

CHRISTIAN HISTORY, Issue 27 entitled "Persecution in the Early Church (1990, Vol. IX, No. 3), page 22.

Joan Carroll Cruz, *EUCHARISTIC MIRACLES* (Rockford, Illinois: TAN Books, 1987).

Cyril, *CATECHETICAL LECTURES*: 22 (Mystagogic 4), 6; Jurgens, page360, #843.

Cyril, *CATECHETICAL LECTURES*: (Mystoagogic 4), 6; Jurgens, page 361, #846.

Ignatius, *LETTER TO THE ROMANS* 7, 3; Jurgens, page 22#54a.

Ignatius, *LETTER TO THE SMYRNAEANS* 6, 2; William Jurgens, *THE FAITH OF THE EARLY FATHERS* (Collegeville, Minn.: Liturgical press, 1970), vol. 1, page 25, #64.

Irenaeus, *AGAINST HERESIES,* 3, 3, 2; Jurgens, page 90, #210.

Irenaeus, *AGAINST HERESIES*, 3, 4, 1; Jurgens, page 90, #213.

Irenaeus, *AGAINST HERESIES*,1, 10, 1; Jurgens, page 19, #45.

Justin Martyr, *FIRST APOLOGY,* 66, 20; Jurgens, page 55, #128.

Father Mitch Pacwa, *EUCHARISTIC SYMBOLS IN THE OLD TESTAMENT* (www.saintjoe.com, 2003).

Lee Strobel, *THE CASE FOR CHRIST: A JOURNALIST'S PERSONAL INVESTIGATION OF THE EVIDENCE FOR JESUS* (Grand Rapids, Mi., 1998).

The St. Paul Center for Biblical Theology, *FROM GENESIS TO JESUS: A JOURNEY THROUGH THE SCRIPTURES* (www.salvationhistory.com), 2003.

Nicholas Cardinal Wiseman *THE REAL PRESENCE OF OUR LORD JESUS IN THE BLESSED EUCHARIST* (London: Burns Oates & Washbourne, 1942).